T0167775

# With
# These
# Hands

# Pam Ayres

## With These Hands

EBURY
PRESS

Ebury Press, an imprint of Ebury Publishing
20 Vauxhall Bridge Road
London SW1V 2SA

Ebury Press is part of the Penguin Random House group of companies
whose addresses can be found at global.penguinrandomhouse.com

Penguin
Random House
UK

Originally published by Weidenfeld & Nicolson in 1997
This edition published by Ebury Press in 2021

www.penguin.co.uk

A CIP catalogue record for this book is available from the British Library

ISBN 9781529104950

Printed and bound in Great Britain by Clays Ltd, Elcograf S.p.A.

The authorised representative in the EEA is Penguin Random House
Ireland, Morrison Chambers, 32 Nassau Street, Dublin D02 YH68.

MIX
Paper from
responsible sources
FSC
www.fsc.org    FSC® C018179

*To D, W & J*

# Contents

# Foreword

It is now twenty-four years since this collection was first published. Saying that makes me feel a bit like Stonehenge, but nevertheless I am delighted to see this new edition.

I wrote these pieces to perform on stage, in most cases in the hope that audiences would find them funny. If you like acting as much as I do, then it is a joy to pretend to be the horrible grasping lottery winner who is going to keep all the money to himself in 'Let It Be Me', the tired mum trying to keep on top of everything in 'With These Hands' or the world-weary observer seeing congregations flock to the supermarket in 'Nowadays We Worship at Saint Tesco'. Performing these pieces, I could stand on the stage and become all these different people, and I loved it.

My great good fortune was that I loved both performing *and* writing, and by combining the two could make a career. It was incredible. After all the early, joyless, clerical jobs, I could make a living doing something I loved and which felt right. Going out on stage terrified me, but I couldn't resist it. The more you overcome that fear and achieve a successful performance, the more confident you feel about the next time. To anyone who longs to perform, I say the more you do it, the more you *can* do it. Honestly. Keep at it!

I could tell you that re-reading this book and being aware of the passage of time makes me feel a little sad, and certainly

I do feel flickers of nostalgia when I read 'Thirteen-Nil' or 'How Can That Be My Baby?' because they were written at a time when our two boys were growing up. What nonsense though, to yearn for the past when I can see our sons as they are now – kind, well-liked men with their own careers, surrounded by their families, my much-loved grandchildren. And I am still married to the same good man. Why on earth would I want the old days back?

Some of these poems surprised me. I didn't expect that 'Yes, I'll Marry You, My Dear' would become a popular reading at weddings, and for a while, when people came up to me and said, 'We had your poem at our wedding!' I didn't know what they meant. How lovely, though, to be a part of such an important day.

'Babe, Won't You Send Me a Fax?' is of course dated, but what a chilling reminder of how cumbersome communication used to be. To think of faxing someone, in these days, when in an instant you can talk face to face on a range of devices.

The overwhelming feeling I have when reading this book, written when I was much younger, is one of incredulity that I was so extraordinarily lucky. I came from a modest background where it was reasonably assumed that I would land some uninspiring job, work for a bit, meet some plodding version of Mr Right, get married, produce unspecified numbers of robust children, have a few boring holidays and disappear without trace. Instead of that, it has been a roller coaster of a life. Not everyone of course, but many people liked my work and shared my sense of humour. Because of them, my books became bestsellers. I travelled the world, took the train through the Rocky Mountains and saw bears at the trackside, I gawped over the edge of the Grand Canyon, explored the beauty of the Australian outback, climbed the Sydney Harbour Bridge, heard the bellbirds of the Abel Tasman National Park in New Zealand, and saw out the old century beneath Table Mountain in Cape Town, South Africa. Honestly, I saw marvels.

Now, with hindsight, I am glad I stuck to my guns. People try to dissuade you when you seek to be different. My wonderful mother, who wanted the best for me, said in her lovely unadulterated Berkshire accent: 'You lives in a world of dreams, my gal.' But they were dreams that came true.

I thank my younger self for having the courage, against all advice, to leave the security of a regular job. For seeking a different job, doing something I loved. I had no idea how it would end; I just felt a strong impulse to write these poems and many others, to produce something new out of my own brain, something to strike a chord with other people and which, if you practiced and worked hard and suffered agonies of stage fright and doubt, might reward you with that roar of laughter from the audience which makes it all worthwhile.

I am writing this foreword at the end of 2020, the year a fearsome pandemic struck, bringing unprecedented sadness and separation. Reading through this earlier work of mine made me smile, and I so hope it does the same for you.

Thank you for liking my work, and I really hope you enjoy this brand-new edition of *With These Hands*.

Pam Ayres, 2020

# Introduction

I had two reasons for starting to write. Firstly I was reckoned to be good at it and liked the praise. Secondly I was eager to try performing something funny on stage, but could find nothing already written which suited either my speech or my sense of humour.

I went to Faringdon Secondary Modern School, and two English teachers stand out from that time. One was Bill Reeves, who encouraged me, laughed at my stories and put them up on the classroom wall. The other, who later became Headmaster of Debenham Modern School in Suffolk, was A. J. Holifield, who listened with due care and solemnity to my hare-brained ideas.

In a drama lesson when I was about twelve, Mr Holifield suggested that we might work on a kind of revue. Straight away I volunteered to do a comic portrayal of Diana Dors, the famous blonde sex-kitten from Swindon. In my father's dim tool shed at home, I spent night after frozen night with raffia and an old stocking top, working to make a wig. Finished at last, it was like the mane of a rather unusual lion. I acquired a pair of black suede shoes with four-inch heels and wrote a funny song. Thus I had the costume and the script. All that was missing was the bottle. I still remember the shameful day when Mr Holifield gently enquired how the song might be coming along. I knew that at home everything was most meticulously prepared, but suddenly the idea of strutting up and down as Diana Dors in front of my stunned classmates was preposterous and I told him I hadn't been able to come up with anything. I think he sensed my inner struggle because he kindly offered me a tape recorder so that I could tape any ideas in solitude, but even this was too much for my strained nerves. The wig, the four-inch heels and the song mouldered at home, denied their moment of glory.

I left Faringdon School aged fifteen. I was considered to have done well when I passed the Civil Service exam and became a clerical assistant at Didcot Depot. Though glad of the congratulations, I found that I hated the work, the monotonous filling-in of identical forms.

Fortunately, for people under the age of sixteen, the Civil Service ran a Further Education Scheme. This meant that every Wednesday I made the long trek up Cowley Road to the Oxford College of Further Education. There I took two English O levels and a Drama Course. I passed both the GCEs and received the Best Drama Student award from the Mayor of Oxford. This was a modest achievement but nevertheless surprising and exciting, as I had always been prepared to accept the view that, as an 11-plus failure, I must be second-rate material. I then started O Level French and History to see if I could do the same again, but meanwhile all was not well at work.

In a streamlining bid, Didcot Depot had been engulfed by the enormous sprawl of Bicester Depot, and it was to Bicester that we now had to travel each day. This was a much longer journey. Every morning my sister Jean and I stood on a wind-blasted T-junction to catch the 6.22 a.m. bus. Clad in a mini skirt in the depths of winter, this was no joke. Even at that hour our kind mother got up early enough to cook us a pan of sausages. We used to eat them wrapped in greaseproof paper as we wretchedly waited for the headlights of the bus to appear.

Various things now happened which caused matters to come to a head. I was desperately in love with a young Welshman in our office and he, unimpressed by the fact that I would have lain down and died for him, went off to work in the brick kilns of Bedford. Yearning for my brick-hearted love, the early mornings and daily form-filling of Bicester Depot now seemed doubly depressing. Additionally, I saw a glamorous, seductive and wholly misleading advert for the Women's Royal Air Force and decided to join. I went off to the recruiting office at Reading and told the recruiting sergeant that I liked drawing. He immediately earmarked me for work as an air photography plotter in a drawing office, and at a stroke condemned me to four years of another job I didn't like and couldn't do.

Soon after my eighteenth birthday I resigned from my job in the Civil Service. My friends, after a whip-round, gave me a handsome Sheaffer pen of a revolutionary design whereby a long nozzle came menacingly out of the nib and sucked up the ink. It was made more tantalising by the fact that it never once worked.

Thus, in April 1965, with my pen and my unquenchable optimism, I set off to join the Women's Royal Air Force. I was posted to RAF Brampton in Huntingdonshire where I was deeply homesick. However, the Services provide good facilities for people interested in sports, further education, singing, drama, and so on, and at Brampton there was an active Theatre Club which I joined. By some stroke of good fortune they were producing a comedy called *Haul for the Shore* set in Cornwall. The woman playing the lead had dropped out and I, with my country accent, was asked to take on the part at ten days' notice. It seemed quite a big part and some application was required to learn it in that time, but I'll *never* forget how the audience laughed, how they applauded at the end, what it was like to feel that feeling when I could have burst with happiness. The god-like figure of our Squadron Leader mounted the stage when the play finished and told the audience how I had stepped in at *such* short notice, and there was enthusiastic applause. I will always remember that night. It was just a small-scale amateur production in a featureless hall, but it was a turning point for me. In that rank-conscious place I learned that laughter cuts through the barriers. I felt that great overwhelming wave of affection that an audience sometimes bestows on a favoured performer, and most importantly of all, I discovered an environment which made me feel I had arrived in the right place, where *at last* I was a round peg in a round hole.

At the age of nineteen I was posted to RAF Seletar in Singapore. Here in the thick treacly heat steamed a world I had never dreamed of. Around the wired-in WRAF accommodation there were clumps of enormous flowered hibiscus, overhead were huge flame trees, and down at our feet gaped shockingly deep monsoon drains. There were monkeys and praying mantis and thin black snakes like bootlaces. In the local markets I was delighted by gaudy treasures to send home. In Singapore city I was terrified by the evil-looking Singapore River as it rolled black, viscous and stinking under the bridge. There were eating stalls to sit at and Nasi Goreng to tackle with chopsticks. It was a long way from eating a paper-wrapped sausage at 6.22 a.m. waiting for the bus to Bicester.

Seletar had a Theatre Club and a Folk Club, both of which I joined. I appeared in several plays but it was the Friday night get-togethers at Seletar Theatre Club which became important to me. On these occasions members of the club would get up on stage to do an impromptu 'turn'. I wanted to do a turn as well, but I could find nothing to declaim which corresponded with my own sense of humour or that, saddled with my country accent, I could put over in a way that worked. So I began to write for myself. I really wanted to write funny songs, but having no musical knowledge I just wrote down the words. They formed a kind of jokey poem. The first poem I wrote was called 'Foolish Brother Luke'. It was about a shaky love affair and was pretty shaky itself. I wrote it so that I, too, could do a Friday night turn. It proved to be the first of quite a lot.

When I left the WRAF in 1969 I missed both performing and the network of places where performance was encouraged. At that time there was a revival of interest in folk singing and I joined a local club. By now I had a modest portfolio of poems and I could play the guitar a little bit. Often there were only a few people at the folk club and so each one would be called upon several times to enchant the others with a song. I used to sing a song and say one of my poems, and over a period these became popular and were quite frequently requested. I noticed that people who laughed at the poems often asked me if they were available to buy and seemed disappointed when they were not. At the folk club we laughed about me publishing a book but as time went on, and as I began to be offered money to sing and perform at other clubs, I did start to wonder about it more seriously.

One evening at our folk club, a sound recordist from BBC Radio Oxford came round recording pieces for the *Folk Programme*, and he recorded some of my material. Soon afterwards I was invited to BBC Radio Oxford, and I recorded for their weekly poetry spot my tragi-comic poem 'The Battery Hen'. This would have been in about 1974. To my unutterable joy, BBC Radio 4 chose the poem for use on their *Pick of the Week* programme. It was also used on *The Farming Programme* and in a coast-to-coast broadcast by the Canadian Broadcasting Corporation, though I never understood why. I was inundated with letters of approval and BBC Radio Oxford offered me a short weekly spot, a poem a week. I used to walk very slowly up the long staircase to BBC Radio Oxford and savour the heady feeling of working for the BBC, towards whom I still feel an intense gratitude. They noticed me, gave me a platform and the chance to shine. They gave me a real reason to write, to sit down in my Witney flat with my ironing board across the arms of my chair to form an executive desk, and to see what I could come up with.

Requests for copies of the poems now began to come in to Radio Oxford in earnest, and like many writers of verse and poetry before me, I tried in vain to interest a publisher in my glittering wares. Without exception they were discouraging. Egged on by piles of letters asking for a book, I set out to produce my own. I typed up the poems, drew a few line drawings of battery hens and suchlike, looked up printers in the telephone directory and traipsed round on foot seeing how much it would cost to produce some sort of slim volume. Eventually I settled on a firm in Oxford, my boyfriend lent me sixty pounds and I ordered five hundred copies. They were not much more than pamphlets really. In what I now regard as an uncharacteristically brave act, I took them round to various bookshops and tried to sell them. It was hard. Great glossy tomes lined the walls as I stood proffering my booklet from a string bag. Yet none of those local bookshop owners refused. They all took some, if only two or three.

In 1975 I won the TV talent show *Opportunity Knocks* with my poem 'Pam Ayres and the Embarrassing Experience with the Parrot' and on Friday 13 February 1976, bolstered by money from a TV advert for artery-clogging cream cheese, I left my job as a shorthand typist and decided to make my way as best I could as a writer and entertainer.

Since then I have worked a great deal in television, radio, and the theatre in this country and abroad. In 1997 I will have published twenty-one books and it is true to say that I love writing just as much now as I did when I wrote that song at school about Diana Dors. I love it because the result is unpredictable. While some days are hopeless, on a good day I sit down to write and from somewhere comes a funny poem, a song that works, a sketch or a story, and it's lovely to have made something new. I never get tired of it. The only time I couldn't write was when our two sons were very young and I, not being in the first flush of youth, felt utterly exhausted. That was the only time that no ideas were forthcoming.

This collection is made up of material I wrote for my one-woman show. I have included, for the first time in a book, the monologues and sketches I use because they are now equally as well received as the poems. Almost everything is written to be read out loud with gusto and a sense of mischief. Happy reading!

*Pam Ayres, 1996*

# With These Hands

With these hands so soft and clean,
On which I stroke the Vaseline,
I soothe the fever, cool the heat,
Lift verrucas out of feet,
Slap the plasters on the knees,
Dig the garden, prune the trees,
And if it doesn't work at all,
I throw the mower at the wall.

With these hands I crack the eggs,
Floss my teeth, shave my legs,
Write the cheques, count the fivers,
Make rude signs at piggish drivers,
Clean the goldfish, light the fires,
Pump up half a dozen tyres,
Feed the hamster, worm the dog
And decorate the Yuletide log.

With these hands I block the lens
When taking photos of my friends,
This is Mary, this is Fred,
See their eyeballs all gone red.
With them I gesticulate,
I wag a finger, say, 'You're late!'
Throw them up, say, 'Don't ask me!'
And, 'What's that in your hand? Let's see!'

With these hands I fondly make,
A brontosaurus birthday cake,
I'm sorry for the shape it's in,
But half of it stuck in the tin.
I pop the corn, I pick the mix,
I whack the cricket ball for six,
I organise the party game,
And clean up things too vile to name.

No pair of jeans do I refuse,
No Levis, Wranglers or FUs,
I wash them fast, I mend them quick,
I sew through denim hard and thick,
For no repair job makes *me* frown,
I take them up, I let them down,
I do the fly, I do the rip,
I do the knee, I do the zip.

And with these hands I dab the eyes,
Officiate at fond goodbyes,
As in the earth we gravely dig
The late lamented guinea pig.
I bow my head, cross my chest,
And lay his furry soul to rest,
Reflecting that, on many a day,
I could have helped him on his way.

I greet the folk who bang the door,
Fill the mouths that shout for more,
Scrape the trainers free of muck,
Gut the fish and stuff the duck,
I cart the shopping, heave the coal,
Stick the plunger down the bowl,
Take foreign bodies from the eye
And with these hands I wave

Goodbye.

# Guppy's Camp

My father worked for the Electricity Board for forty-four years and got a clock. It had what they called a Westminster Chime, which is to say that it chimed every quarter of an hour, very soothing in the middle of the night. As the youngest of a family of six children, I never knew what it was to go without the essentials, but it was a long time before our parents felt we could afford a luxury like a proper holiday where we went away for a whole week. When that time finally came we greeted it with huge excitement and joy.

Even if we'd wanted to, and it would not have meant committing the offence of looking 'out of place', we could not have gone anywhere smart or expensive like Budleigh Salterton or Lyme Regis. Instead we went to a spot along the coast from Weymouth in Dorset. This was a caravan site called Guppy's Camp. We had no prior knowledge of it but had seen an advert in the newspaper. It said, 'Four-berth caravan, Guppy's Camp, Private Facilities'. The Private Facilities appealed to our snobby instincts. We thought this would place it a cut above all the other four-berth caravans, which just goes to show how wrong you can be, because when we arrived we found the Private Facilities were nothing more than four sheets of corrugated iron, without the refinement of a roof, lashed together over a precipitous drop.

My sister and I soon discovered that once Mum or Dad had entered the Private Facilities and fastened the sophisticated hasp and staple closure, we could stand next to the ramshackle structure and rock the whole thing backwards and forwards on its axis. The poor, trapped victim clung on within and shouted blood-curdling threats, but could not get out to enact them. This pastime was a popular diversion for my sister and myself, but, for the most part, every day followed the same pattern as, in a number of set stages, we made our way to the beach.

First we would get up, and this in itself was no simple matter. The original advert had claimed that bedding was provided for a family of four. This was not the case. After much fruitless searching for plump bales of blankets, my mother discovered a few threadbare and pitiful rags slung on the damp planks of the wardrobe floor. These were alleged to be the bedding. Our parents were horrified. They kindly put what there was on our bed and then made do themselves. Their bed let down out of the wall and they made it up using coats, cardigans, tea towels, and so on. On the first night they

were very cold and Dad remembered that during the war, in Germany, in freezing conditions, the soldiers had put layers of newspaper into their clothing for extra insulation. He therefore set to and interleaved their makeshift bedclothes with sheets of the *Daily Mirror*. This did indeed keep them warmer, but as they thrashed about restlessly the loud rustling drove us mad. Interestingly, they would go to bed white, and rise up black from the newsprint.

Our mother would then cook us a good breakfast. Fat was not considered a threat to health then and half a packet of lard would shoot across the hot frying pan to get things going. The cramped caravan would fill with a blue haze and the sound of fried eggs wallowing.

As we ate, Mum would lay out a series of carrier bags and fill each one with a different category of item to be taken to the beach. There were no facilities or amenities of any kind on the beach and so whatever you thought you were going to need you had to take yourself. Mum would patiently pack each bag and lean it against the wall of the caravan.

Into the first bag went all the swimming stuff – towels, costumes, talcum powder and those white rubber hats that twisted your face round to one side. My hat always seemed to have perished. I would get hold of the sharp metal buckle, give it a good long stretch, and it would come off in my hand.

Into the second bag went everything that might be needed in the event of foul weather. This formed a giant heap, including coats, cardigans, macs, the umbrella, Mum's plastic concertina rain-hat and the windbreak. This was a piece of striped canvas with stakes stitched into it, complete with mallet. Dad used to spend ages on the beach deciding on the optimum position for the windbreak, thrusting a sucked finger into the air and angling the thing just so. It would then be driven ferociously into the sand with the mallet, the whole family plus baggage would settle comfortably behind it and then the wind would completely change direction and come from somewhere else.

The next bag contained everything we might need to eat and drink because on the beach at Guppy's Camp there were no shops, you couldn't even get a cup of tea. This bag had the sandwiches, the crisps, the flask and, from the local pub, a bottle of terrifyingly pink cherryade which I confidently believe had never once seen a cherry. Also adding its considerable weight to this bag was a thing which my sister and I used to dread. The cake. Mum used to make it at home and bring it wrapped in greaseproof paper. You'd see other people on the beach with the angel cake you could get from Woolworth's. It had pink and yellow layers sandwiched up with cream. Ours wasn't like that. Ours was a hard, round, brown, mean-looking cake, flavoured with either currants or caraway seeds, and it made a point of lasting the whole week no matter how many slices you prised off it. It was always exceedingly dry. I don't know how my mother mastered the technique of making it so reliably dry, but you needed a bucket of water to wash it down.

The next bag contained things for people to do – the occupational therapy. Into that went Dad's racing paper so that he could study the form, the *Daily Mirror* and Mum's knitting, as she was always making a great voluminous cardigan for someone who didn't want it.

Finally, there was a small but crucially important bag containing things we might need in the event that disaster struck. The first item in it was the blue bag, the Reckitt's Blue. This made an annual pilgrimage from the wash-house to the seaside and back again and was included in case anyone got stung. I always used to get stung, I think it was due to the jam in our sandwiches. It was blackberry and apple and you could see the wasps coming over from the Isle of Wight. When any of us were stung Mum would sprint down to the water's edge, damp the blue bag in the sea and press it firmly against the affected area for some minutes. To my certain knowledge, this ritual made no difference whatsoever to the pain, but did make the affliction a great deal easier to see.

The other item in that bag was a tube of a pink substance called Algipan, still available today. Described as a Warming Rub, we took it along because my father had undergone the removal from his knee of what he always referred to as 'the cartridge'. Father's knee used to flare up. I grew up thinking it was an incendiary device which might at any time explode in a sheet of flame. It flared up at the least provocation, particularly if Mother had asked him to do something to help her, and it would then need to be anointed with the Algipan.

This then was the baggage, and when it was assembled all four members of the party, Mum, Dad, my sister Jean and myself, would grasp two bags each and walk along the crunching cinder path to the beach. Progress was slow. Heavily laden, like refugees we would trudge through the countless caravans, through the pong of everyone else's frying bacon, until at last the little path widened and there we were, finally, triumphantly, on the beach.

It was such a thrill for Jean and me. Of course we had been on day trips before when the bus came and took you home in the evening, but for us to stand there by the sea, knowing we could come back tomorrow, and the day after, and the day after that, was a joy beyond words. On the last day, when we had to go home, my sister and I clutched each other and cried. However, given the passage of time a perspective can change, and as I look back now certain aspects of the holiday make my hair stand on end.

The beach left a lot to be desired. It was not a nice golden, sandy beach, but more of a grey grit. It lacerated your feet. This could be controlled by donning a pair of the giant plimsolls discarded by our brothers, but they were not a popular option as they were hard to keep on and detracted from the stylishness of the wearer.

On the left-hand side of the beach there was a pillbox, one of the squat fortifications put up during the war. Round and immensely strong, it was made of concrete and brick with a series of slitty windows round its circumference and an entrance at the back. This was so the soldiers could go in and stick their guns through the slitty windows had the Germans decided to invade Guppy's Camp, which fortunately they hadn't. It was therefore a redundant building which, in the absence of a public convenience, tended to serve a dual purpose.

On the far side of the beach was the one thing which drew my sister and me like a magnet. On our arrival we used to drop the bags and rush over to play there all day. It was the one place we yearned to be, beside a long, white sewage-outflow pipe which ran down the length of the beach. It was round and fat and bolted together in sections. You could sit astride it, pretend it was a horse and feel the sea foaming round your legs. We would leap from it into the water and it was ideal for all sorts of imaginary games. A cloudy sort of warm water used to issue from it at low tide and my sister and I, not knowing what it was, used to dam it up and play with it and frolic in the froth. When I think about this now, it amazes me that we didn't catch some dread disease.

One photograph survives from that holiday. It is a snapshot of the four of us on the beach and from the various backdrops available we have selected the sewage pipe. We are all lined up against it, wearing the swimming costumes of the day. In the case of my mother, my sister and myself, this was a ruched swimming costume, elasticated all over in squares. For variety they were all navy blue, and at the front each one was hitched up higher on one side than the other. This was because of the complicated system of straps. Two of them needed to be taken up, crossed at the back of the neck, brought round the side and fed through two minuscule loops, hard to find if your hands were freezing cold and encrusted with sand. Then, straps held well out to the sides, you had to fling yourself forwards and tie them securely across your back. If, at the end of this performance, the front of the costume was not quite level, you were past caring. Another thing I remember about those ruched swimming costumes was that even though you had taken them off, you remained beautifully ruched for some hours afterwards.

Of course my father was not wearing a ruched swimming costume. He was wearing a swimming costume which my mother had actually knitted for him. Many dads on the beach wore similarly stylish garments. Dad's was worked in garter stitch from a pattern in the *Woman's Weekly*. Threaded through the waist and clearly visible was white knicker elastic, tied at the front in a giant knot.

The only thing I didn't like about Dad's swimming costume was the colour. It was a shade of ginger, like mustard found after too long in the fridge. Nevertheless I thought this was a great achievement, a hand-knitted swimming costume, and without doubt it was a very snug fit on Father. He was a fine, good-looking man, an ex-Grenadier Guardsman, tall and erect with a natty little Clark Gable moustache. When he walked up and down the beach he must have been aware of the eyes upon him because the ginger swimming costume certainly enhanced his contours.

As long as it was dry.

Once it got wet the whole situation changed. Wool has a great capacity to absorb water and when wet the whole edifice used to drop. Father would walk into the sea looking splendid and walk out looking like the monster from the Black Lagoon, with a great bulging gusset full of water. It looked obscene. It was so heavy that Father would have to reach down and give it a bit of support. He could not walk. You would see him clutching the waterlogged mass, looking round furtively for inspiration. Then he would spot the pillbox and make for it crab-fashion across the beach. There he could be seen, a crouched figure, wringing the Weymouth brine from his gusset.

My next poem is about the seaside. I wrote it because last summer my husband, our two sons and I went on holiday together to another seaside town far from Weymouth. After the long hot journey I took the boys out to run joyfully on the beach. One of them picked up an item which he believed to be a cuttlefish. It was white but it was no cuttlefish. I won't elaborate, but on closer inspection the beautiful beach was found to be dotted with similar items. It was very polluted and dirty. I found this a small but deeply depressing experience, after which I could cheerfully have gone straight home. It did however give me the idea for my poem, which takes an undoubtedly rose-coloured view of the seaside as I first knew it in the fifties and a more jaundiced view of it as it is today.

# *The Seaside*

## (Or Coastal Erosion)

I used to like the seaside. I don't go much any more,
There's been a subtle change in what you find along the
    shore,
I'm gazing at the water and with dread my toes have curled,
As I think of people eating fibre all around the world.


Here beside the ocean I am staring at the scene,
From underneath another coat of SPF 15,
I watch the tankers pass, they look so sinister and black,
This morning here's the front, and then tonight ...
                                        there goes the back.

A hundred thousand walkers with their marching boots
    and packs,
Are tramping round the cliffs admiring one another's backs,
The narrow coastal path, alas, has cracked beneath the load,
And fallen in the water, so you'll have to take the road.

Little local restaurants are nestled side by side,
McDonald's, Pizza Hut, a Burger King, Kentucky Fried,
This is where the kids enjoy a saturated meal
And hang around arcades where life is virtually real.

I used to buy the seaside rock and take my friends a stick,
I used to have a seaside hat emblazoned 'Kiss me Quick!'
A mercury thermometer with lighthouses and ships,
But now I get my mercury from plates of fish and chips.

I caught a fish this morning! But I threw it back instead,
Well it was rather small. And radioactive. It was dead.
For now along the waterline, all that can be heard,
Is the slap of oily water on a decomposing bird.

Once we'd walk along the quay and buy a herring or a sole,
Not any more. Our fishermen are queuing for the dole.
But here comes the Armada and they offer thanks to God,
As they shout, '*Viva España*' and hoover up the cod.

There's gangs around the shops and I'm afraid I might be
    mugged.
There's gangs along the beach and I'm afraid they might
    be drugged,
They're making funny noises now from underneath the pier,
I don't know what they're doing. But I've got a good idea.

I'd like to take a photograph to show that I was there,
But my camera's been nicked, I left it hanging on the chair,
So I'm walking to the station and I'm getting on the train,
I used to like the seaside: but I shan't go there again.

# Seletar

I left school at the age of fifteen unencumbered by educational qualifications of any kind and I sat the Civil Service examination, passing it by one mark. At that time the choices for girls like me were fairly limited. Many of my friends went into some kind of light industrial assembly work, or they went as machinists to a manufacturer of military uniforms in Swindon. I did not know anybody else who was going into the Civil Service, or what to expect when I got there. I was aware that people were pleased with me, that I had succeeded in getting a 'sit-down job' when the alternative meant you stood up all day and got varicose veins.

I started work then, as a clerical assistant, in a place called the Central Ordnance Depot, Didcot. I have to say it lacked glamour. It issued Army units with military stores and materials and, though it supplied no weaponry, it did seem to stock everything else. When an Army unit required blankets, oil stoves, canteens of cutlery, hexagonal bolts, countersunk screws, flanges or grommets of any description, they would fill in a requisition and send it to Didcot. There it was laboriously processed by a team of ladies including myself, seated at long lines of tables in an office as large as an aircraft hangar. Gradually each requisition would work its way along the table. The lady next to me would stamp it with a big rubber stamp, and my job from the time I was fifteen to the time I was seventeen was to write two noughts in the top right-hand corner. As you can imagine, this was a deeply satisfying job. At the end of two years it was driving me nuts.

To relieve the excruciating boredom I used to take two romantic magazines. One was called *Valentine* and the other was *Roxy*, and they were concerned with such breathless issues as would she get him or not? Would they make it to the back row of the pictures or would her hopes be DASHED?

One day I was looking through one of my magazines when I came across something which did actually change my life. I know this sounds dramatic but it did. It was a full-page advert designed to persuade young women to join the Women's Royal Air Force. Up to that moment I'd had no thought of a military career at all, nothing was further from my mind, but this advert was very seductive indeed. I can still see it now. The central figure was a young woman, not dissimilar to myself, my sort of age and build but with a dramatic difference. She looked radiantly happy. She was wearing the tropical uniform of the Women's Royal Air Force, a natty little creamy dress with epaulettes, cinched in at the waist. She had on the little hat set at a jaunty angle, her chest was thrown out and she was saluting. She was a picture of radiant happiness. Clearly she had no thoughts of noughts in top right-hand corners. Moreover she was surrounded by things that hinted of dark excitement. As I feverishly scanned the picture I could not fail to take in the clump of palm trees quivering in the breeze, the jet aircraft pointing dramatically up at the sky and, standing all around her in a semicircle, smouldering, a group of the most devastatingly handsome pilots you had ever seen, all staring down at her with undisguised lust. There didn't seem to be much comparison really. In the spring of 1965 I rushed off to a recruiting office in Reading and joined.

They sent me off to Grantham, to the piquantly named RAF Spitalgate. The first thing I noticed was a marked lack of the things in the picture. Over Spitalgate no palm trees waved. On seeing me, what few men there were did not seem to have to grapple with their primitive urges, and furthermore there was not a single aircraft to be seen. I had been diddled.

Fortunately I did not stay too long in Grantham, and to my delight in 1967 I was posted to RAF Seletar in Singapore. For a country girl like me who had never travelled beyond the Blackpool hallucinations, it was an utter revelation. It seemed like a miracle. The bright sunshine, the colours, the jungly swamps, the coconut palms, the chameleon on the bush where I ate my sandwiches at lunchtime: seeing these things was like waking up from a grey dream and seeing vibrant life for the first time. I loved the place. I was frightened of it, but I did love it.

RAF Seletar had an active and thriving Theatre Club, which I joined. It had marvellous facilities, a fine theatre and a clubroom with veranda and rattan furniture. I suppose the Theatre Club staged four or five plays a year, I can't remember now. I know I tried to be in as many of them as possible. What I recall more clearly were the Friday night Club Nights, when the members would meet for a bit of a get-together. They would have a drink and a laugh, and a Chinese man would come round selling satay, bits of spiced meat on sticks which you dabbled in a puddle of sauce on your plate. You can get it in Waitrose now, but then it seemed very foreign and exotic.

As the evening wore on the membership would start to feel the need for a bit of entertainment and people would get up on stage and do a bit of a 'turn', a party piece of some kind. This took a wondrous variety of forms. Some people would take it quite seriously and perform a piece from Shakespeare. Then there were two men who used to stand one in front of the other and give a spine-chilling rendition of 'There's a one-eyed yellow idol to the north of Khatmandu' with the other one at the back doing the arm movements. Another man had an amazing act. He would come on stage with a bucket of water and a tape recorder. He switched on the tape whereupon the audience was assailed by the sound of a dramatic roll of drums. As this reached a mighty climax, he would do no more than lift up and drink the entire bucket of water. This was the act. He would then switch off the tape recorder and walk off … in some haste. You can see that these were evenings of sophisticated entertainment.

From my point of view the thing about them was that I used to sit in the audience and long to get up on stage and do something too. I felt sure I could, if only I could find the right material. I scoured all kinds of humorous books, listened to funny records and couldn't find a thing that felt right for me to say. These circumstances were what made me start writing. It was at Seletar that I first stood quaking on the stage and offered the dubious audience a piece of comic verse which I had written myself. It was a feeble piece entitled 'Foolish Brother Luke'. They laughed. I went from there.

# The Celluloid Man

I wish I could find for I'm terribly keen,
The kind of young man that you see on the screen,
I've searched on my own but concluded I fear
That there simply aren't any at all around here.

Yet I see him so clear: in his bottle-green coat,
His dark curly hair and the lace at his throat,
The smouldering aspect, the curl of his lip,
His boots of fine leather, his gloves, and his whip.

At the lake edge where night-scented flowers commune
He is deep in the shadows and lit by the moon,
I breathlessly see him step forward and wait
And under my bonnet my ringlets go straight.

I see his dark features suffusing with lust,
As with stark admiration he squints at my bust,
With candlelight only to lighten the black
At the inn he can take me to Heaven and back.

Not by carriage or coach, no by nothing like that,
On a massive great stallion as black as your hat,
On clattering cobbles it plunges and moves
In showers of sparks from its massive great hooves.

Charging like Pegasus over the gorse.
Me and the man and the night and the horse.
I *know* he is out there, so noble and fine.
On BBC2 at a quarter past nine.

I wish Fate would show some compassion to me,
I want a REAL man like I see on TV,
I'll wait where the night-scented flowers commune
At the edge of the lake: by the light of the moon.

# I Loved an Antique Dealer

I loved an antique dealer,
I loved him heart and soul,
Although he was bow-fronted,
And his legs were cabriole,
His eyes they were cross-banded,
And his surface was distressed,
But he was nicely moulded,
With a sturdy little chest.

But on examination,
There were several things he lacked,
I found him dummy-fronted,
And I found him spindle-backed,
So I sent him off to auction,
And I've had a note from there,
To say he's on a pedestal,
In Weston-super-Mare.

# Grannies and Gyms

Have you noticed how much grannies have changed? I have. I grew up in the fifties, in a council house in a row on the village green, and each one of those council houses contained a granny belonging to one side of the family or the other. While some of the grannies were still fairly roadworthy, I think it's fair to say that the majority were in quite an advanced state of decay. As children we were always in and out of each other's houses and somehow the grannies all looked the same. They sat in the same position, on the right-hand side of the kitchen range, out of the draught, but not so far over that they blocked the entrance to the cupboard. They all wore drab colours, brown or grey or some mouldy-looking tweed. I used to think they were entirely interchangeable: you could swap one family's granny with another and nobody would ever notice the difference.

When we talked to a granny we always used a great loud voice that hurt your throat because we would automatically assume she was as deaf as a post. We said what we had to say in a painfully slow, exaggerated fashion with much pronounced trumpet-like movement of the mouth, which we then assumed she could lip-read. Understandably, a lot of the grannies ignored us completely. They used to knit. They made a lot of those crinoline women you pull over toilet rolls to beautify them. As we enunciated before the hunched grannies, they knitted more feverishly than ever. A few would look up and acknowledge us, one might even give us a smile, whereupon we could observe that she had some teeth, or no teeth, or just the one pickle-stabber in the front.

What you would not think at any stage was, 'There is a woman with prospects.' You wouldn't think the old lady had much to look forward to and, frankly, neither would she. You'd think that whatever she was going to get, she'd had. Thankfully this is no longer the case. Today older women are out in the workplace, doing demanding jobs and looking good. Banished at last is the terrible old put-down 'mutton dressed as lamb', sharply applied to any no-longer-youthful woman trying to make the best of herself. Modern women like make-up and use it skilfully, their hair looks good and they dress well. I think all this is terrific. I believe the change in older women is due to many factors, but I would like to touch briefly on three.

Firstly, nutrition. We are all better informed about it, we know what to eat and what vitamins and minerals we need to keep ourselves fighting fit. Reliable information is freely available and women take advantage of it.

Secondly, and a great boon to countless women: HRT. Husband Replacement Therapy.

Thirdly, exercise. We know about the benefits to be gained from keeping fit and are aware that just three twenty-minute exercise sessions a week can go a long way towards keeping us healthy and mobile. Exercise is on offer everywhere. Gyms have sprung up like mushrooms in many towns and numerous council-run sports centres have gyms available as well. These are wholesome gyms, oriented not towards the teeth-gritted, sweat-drenched, no-gain-without-pain brigade, nor like the inner-city gyms of my youth where people like

Henry Cooper went to beat other people to a pulp, but fun places offering fitness for the whole family.

A year or two ago my husband and I joined a gym. It was just after Christmas and we had eaten too much. Suddenly our clothes were too tight and our waistbands cut in. Opening newspapers or magazines we were poleaxed by adverts from slimming operations posing questions like 'Have you got Orange Peel Thighs? Are you Happy With Your Body?' We felt sheepish and guilty.

We live near an area of worked-out gravel pits which are currently being put to new use. One has been taken over by the Education Authority and is used as a centre to teach water-based activities like canoeing, sailing and snorkelling. Another has been declared a nature reserve, entirely enclosed in a tall fence and left alone to see what colonises it: rats, things like that. A third has been trimmed with a border of holiday cottages and equipped with a gym. At that time the gym had just opened and was offering a reduced membership fee for people who joined early. My husband and I decided to investigate. It was very smart. It held out the promise of transforming us from the overweight and gluttonous to the confident and well-toned. We joined in the January and left in the February.

First of all we were assessed. My husband had to go off with a man and I was taken into a cubicle by a young woman. She was size ten, aged eighteen and clad in a saintly little white frock. I was fat and fortyish and I'm sure if I was a nicer person she would not have grated on me in the way she did.

She had a notebook, a pencil and a pair of callipers. With her thumb and finger she pinched my fatty bits and measured their thickness with the callipers. I expect I have felt more humiliated before but I can't remember when it was. With these measurements she was able to calculate how much of my body weight was made up of fat. Next she took my pulse, writing down the result in the notebook. She then made me get on an exercise bike and pedal it like a madwoman for eight minutes, after which she took my pulse again. There was a dramatic difference between the two readings. With these and other nefarious tests she was able to build up a picture of my physical fitness, such as it was. She then devised a programme of exercise for me to follow once I went into the gym itself, and in my Tesco tracksuit I entered the arena.

I was assailed by several things and I didn't like any of them. The first one was the smell. The place was properly ventilated and air-conditioned, but nevertheless people appeared to be strapped round the walls performing difficult movements while in agony. They wore a uniform of drenched grey marl and in the air was that smell of fresh sweat so terrifying to the unexercised.

Secondly, I did not like the sound effects. Loud unexpected shouts and barks came at me from all round the gym, agonised bellows reminiscent of the last crucifying stages of childbirth. I was discomfited. I did not know where to look.

Thirdly, I did not feel attuned to the contraptions. Squat, hard and black-and-white, they ranged round the room with names like Pec Deck, Lat Pulldown, Chest Press or Leg Curl. These titles had the effect of making me feel like an outsider. I did not want my chest pressed or my leg curled. I was unnerved and filled with foreboding.

A large man with spread legs was strapped into the Pec Deck. When my saintly companion saw him, her face became suffused with light. This, she confided, was a person I would see frequently, he was a professional weightlifter and worked out in the gym three or four times a week! He was a fellow member: I would have a friend!

'Let me introduce you', she trilled, 'to Spike!'

Sometimes you look at people, don't you? Sometimes you look at certain people and quietly to yourself think 'No'. Well, I looked at Spike as he laboured, this perspiring mountain of flesh with oiled legs, great shining eyes and an overshot jaw. I looked at Spike and I thought 'No'.

I was taken round the various pieces of equipment and they were demonstrated to me. I was shown how to crouch at the back of each machine and adjust it to suit my own ability. This involved a column of clunking weights behind smoked glass. As I crouched there, adjusting the knob, I had the creeping feeling that all this wasn't me. This crystallised into certainty in front of a machine called Adduction. This was a new word to me. I looked it up in the dictionary and it means 'to draw together to a common centre'. I will try to explain it to you by first describing the Pec Deck, which works in a similar way.

The Pec Deck has a seat for you to sit on and two black pads at shoulder level. You have to place a hand behind each black pad and press them together so that they meet in the centre. This is made more strenuous than it sounds because the pads are weighted to resist you. You have to press them hard to get them together and then you have to resist them as they come back, otherwise your hands clap round the back of your head. Correctly done, these movements exercise and tone the muscles of the chest.

The Adduction machine works on a similar principle. Here you sit on a shallow seat and at the sides there are black handles for you to grasp. Although it has two black pads like the Pec Dec, they are not at shoulder height. These are between the knees. What happens is that you sit down, grip the black handles and the two pads wrench your knees apart. Wide apart. This is a terrible shock if you are not expecting it. What you then have to do is force your knees back together. This open-and-shut action forms the exercise. It is strenuous to do and corrects any flabbiness of the inner thigh.

I did not like it.

I was modestly brought up to sit with the knees chastely together, to cross the legs discreetly at the ankle, to smooth the skirt respectably down over the thighs. This yanking apart of the legs was more than I or the Tesco tracksuit could take, particularly as I on my machine was placed directly opposite the grunting Spike on his. I got off, and walked as best I could to the next one.

At first I felt cheered. It was a rowing machine. I have done bits of fun rowing and I thought I could probably cope with this machine better than all the others. It had a large flywheel arrangement at one end and a little seat at the other. This was a very little seat about as big as the lid of an individual Christmas pudding, and when I sat on it there was an unflattering and unsupported surplus. You then only had to secure your feet to the footplates with a thick Velcro strap before leaning forwards and manfully seizing the bar representing the oars. In doing this I noticed a scrappy handwritten notice affixed to the wall with Blu-Tack. It said, 'Please wipe your sweat off the handlegrips', and adjacent to it was a giant roll of blue industrial paper. I dabbed at the tacky rubber with twists of paper. Ready at last, I hauled the bar back towards me in a rowing motion, the flywheel hummed and the little seat shot forwards. It was all computerised. A small screen measured the effort expended and told you how many knots or fathoms or whatever it was you would have travelled if the thing hadn't been bolted to the floor. It was deeply strenuous. Soon a searing pain shot across my midriff and I crumpled forwards for a breather, looking to my right, down what I thought was the length of the gym. On closer inspection it was not a continuation of the room at all but a wall made up of a giant mirror disguised at the edge with potted palms. So not only did I suspect that I looked an awful fool, but I could look in the mirror and have it confirmed. I shall never forget what I looked like slumped on the preposterous little seat, my hair hanging in sweaty ropes and my face a bright boiling red. I thought to myself, 'What are you doing here? Are you getting anything at all out of this? No.'

I went home. I just knew it wasn't the place for me. I packed my little sports bag which I had only used the once and left. On my way out there were pleasant-looking women, many of them considerably older than me, having a nice time on the jogging machines. They were firm, well-toned women wearing natty sweat-bands, running and laughing with their friends, and I envied them, but I couldn't do it. I can still hear the swing doors brushing together behind me as I walked out, a total gymnastic flop.

When I arrived home I sat around dejectedly. I had lost my money. I couldn't do it, couldn't cut the mustard, couldn't work out three times a week and reap the benefits. I felt an oaf. Nobody can wallow in self-reproach for ever though, and after a time I began to feel a sense of rebellion, a rising spirit of defiance. This is what led me to write the poem 'Will I Have to Be Sexy at Sixty?' which is in defence of non-participants.

# Will I Have to Be
# Sexy at Sixty?

Will I have to be sexy at sixty?
Will I have to keep trying so hard?
Well I'm just going to slump,
With my dowager's hump
And watch myself turn into lard.

I'm not going to keep exercising,
I'm not going to take HRT,
If a toy boy enquires
I'll say, 'Hah! Hard luck squire!
Where were you in '73!'

I'm not going to shave my moustaches,
I'm just going to let them all sprout,
My chins'll be double
All covered in stubble,
I'm going to become an Old Trout!

My beauty all gone and forgotten,
Vanished with never a quibble,
I'll sit here and just
Kind of gnaw at a crust
And squint at the telly, and dribble.

As my marbles get steadily fewer,
Must I battle to keep my allure?
Have I still got to pout
Now my teeth have come out
And my husband has found pastures newer?

Farewell to the fad and the fashion,
Farewell to the young and the free!
My passion's expired,
At bedtime … I'm TIRED!
Sexy and sixty? Not me!

# *Babe, Won't You Send Me a Fax?*

## A Song

Oh babe, won't you send me a fax,
And finally let me relax,
One piece of paper to crumple and stroke,
And fondle at night like a sensuous bloke
Whose basso profundo's reduced to a croak,
Babe, won't you send me a fax?

I've had about all I can take,
What new sacrifice must I make?
For in my endeavours to earn you a crust,
Far from your side I am tortured with lust,
As sure as I stand here I'll have it or bust,
Babe, won't you send me a fax?

Oh babe, won't you send me a fax,
If only to paper the cracks,
Don't be afraid that you'll lose my respect,
Like a bold horse I am lathered and flecked,
So here is my number to send it direct,
Babe, won't you send me a fax?

By terrible dreams I am tricked,
I dream that the switch has been flicked,
A fax! It's a fax! With no shred of a doubt!
But I reach the machine and the paper's run out
And I fall on the floor too exhausted to shout:
Babe, won't you send me a fax?

Here by the light of the moon
I sit and I feel a poltroon,
I watched in despair as it waned and it waxed,
All of my hopes have been brutally axed
Due to the fact that I haven't been faxed!
Oh babe, won't you send me a FAX!

I tried to find out where you've been,
Left messages on your machine,
Your portable phone I have endlessly rung,
I'm wealthy, I'm lively, I'm handsome, I'm young,
A terrible liar but very well sprung,
Oh babe, won't you send me a fax!

Oh baby, you give me the urge
To finally see it emerge
Hot off the presses, I'll know it's from you,
And right at the bottom of page two of two,
Could you please tell it to say, 'I love you?'
Oh babe, won't you send me,
Oh please, won't you send me,
Oh babe, won't you send me a FAX?

# Searching for Bryan Brown

Across this land I love the best,
From the gold fields of the west,
Through the rolling spinifexes,
As they blow and as they twirl,
I search the endless cane,
And the mighty fields of grain,
For the oyster of Australia,
Has yielded up a pearl.

Through the savage roar of town,
I have searched for Bryan Brown,
I have traced his fleeing footsteps,
On the silent forest floor,
To glimpse his form heroic,
I have plodded ever stoic,
To Katherine, Kalgoorlie,
And the mighty Nullarbor.

By his outfit shall ye know him,
Drizabones shall swing below him,
In a genuine Akubra,
With the marks of battle scored,
In my dreams I go to meet him,
Through the gums I run to greet him,
Straight across the lightly trampled
Form of Rachel Ward.

Is he down at Naracoorte,
Where the life is hard and short,
And over the Merinos is he studiously bent,
Where the shearing shed is rank,
And the wool is warm and dank,
And sheep mill in confusion,
As they wonder where it went?

Is he whipping up a flurry,
Paddle-steaming up the Murray,
To Morgan or Mildura,
Where the river sweetly sings,
Is he droving on the plain,
Is he slashing at the cane,
Or playing ocarina
In a town like Alice Springs?

Oh the films in which I've seen him,
Wished my husband could have been him,
Like the setting sun his image
Slowly fadeth from the plain,
And the spirit of the bush,
And the grin upon his mush,
Are luring me to go
And try to find him once again.

# Keeping Chickens

I don't keep chickens any more, although I did for a while when our children were small. I kept them for two reasons, firstly because I would know the eggs produced were from birds humanely kept and wholesomely fed, and secondly, when one of the hens went broody, I intended to give her a clutch of fertile eggs to sit on. This would enable our children to see the chicks hatch, a charming and educational experience, and the whole family could enjoy watching the mother hen cluck round the garden with her family. This is what I hoped.

I wanted to recreate some of the excitement I had felt myself, long ago in Stanford-in-the-Vale, when my mother used to send away for day-old chicks. They came by train in a stout square box perforated with round holes. Mum would call us in, the box would be on the kitchen table, and she would say, 'Hark! What can you hear?' Through the silence would come the magical cheep-cheep from the box and there would be huge excitement as the little chicks were taken out and stroked and inspected. My sister and I used to take a hammer and bash up wheat for them on the front doorstep. This made a nutritious mixture of crushed wheat and stone dust.

We always had chickens at Stanford, as long as I can remember. At bedtime Mum would put a blackened saucepan on the embers of the fire and this would be left to simmer overnight. Into it went all the potato peelings, small 'pig taters' and various other food scraps under a stout lid. In the morning this was strained, mashed with layer's meal from the grain merchants, and enriched with a shake of fiery pepper which was supposed to make the hens lay. One of my four brothers was sent off to the chickens' run to give them their breakfast. I can see him now staggering up the frost-white grass path, the black saucepan issuing clouds of steam. My mother would watch him go with satisfaction. 'That'll warm 'em,' she'd say. You can see that this is a nice memory for me, I like it, I'm glad to have it and I wanted to create a little bit of something similar for my own family.

It was not so easy. It used to be simple to buy the chickens you wanted. I remember running my fingers down the poultry section of the classified adverts and seeing plenty of entries for our sort of birds. It would say RIR X LS and to the chicken-literate this meant a cross between a brown bird called the Rhode Island Red and a whitish one called the Light Sussex. This combination gave you a personable girl who, given plenty of encouragement and mother's mash, would lay well.

I couldn't find any. Not a single RIR X LS anywhere. In the intervening years chicken breeding has become much more scientific. Commercial egg producers, with some justification, do not want birds which go broody. Going broody means that they stop laying and sit tight on any eggs they can find. To the businessman this represents loss of production and so the bird most frequently offered nowadays is a thing called the Black Rock. In my opinion the Black Rock is a non-chicken. It is not the rich conker-brown of the Rhode Island Red, who has great feathery knickers down her legs and a knowing eye. It is a vile plum colour like claret and mud. It is a machine. It has no maternal instinct. It has a computer-programmed sort of look in its eye. It turns up, fires out the eggs, exhausts itself and keels over, whereupon the businessman ships in some more. I looked at the Black Rock and thought, 'No way, mush,' and resolved to look further afield.

My search took me to a superior sort of establishment which bred and offered for sale old traditional breeds of farm animals, pigs, sheep and particularly poultry. They had all manner of ducks and fancy turkeys. They had geese and guinea fowl. They had Rhode Island Reds and I bought six. The cost was prohibitive. I had to put my name on a long waiting list. It was like ordering one of those posy dogs which real dogs laugh at.

At last the chickens arrived. I had bought a house and all the equipment. I had natty galvanised hoppers for the food, hygienic drinkers, quantities of the proper grit they need for rock-hard eggshells and the finest additive-free feed from a joint twelve miles away in Tetbury. These chickens were feather bedded.

I put them into their quarters and wafted away, happy. Wafting back I found one had a bad leg. She was standing in the corner of the run, wearing an imploring look and holding the gammy leg up in her feathers. I examined it and clearly she was unable to put one foot to the ground at all. As they had cost so much I thought it worth taking her to the vet. I put her under my arm and knocked on the door of his surgery. He manipulated the bird's joint and agreed that it was inflamed. He gave an anti-inflammatory injection to her and a substantial bill to me. I took the chicken home but she did not get better. This took the gloss off the operation a little.

More gloss came off shortly afterwards when another bird fell sick. Now, on her head a chicken should have a nice glossy red comb which sticks up proudly and shines with rude health. If the comb flops over and turns grey this is a sign that you've got problems. A second stricken chicken emerged. Not only did she have a grey, flabby-looking comb like a slab of old bacon, but her breathing was noisy and tormented. I picked her up and we stared at each other, eye to eye. Each rattling and agonised breath seemed likely to be her last. In my hands she was hot and limp. I took her to the vet as well.

'Where did you get these chickens?' he demanded as if they were something nasty from under the counter.

I told him.

I'm beginning to think you might have something viral in your flock,' he said. 'You're not thinking of breeding from these birds, are you?'

'No,' I lied.

'Because I couldn't recommend it at all.'

'Great,' I thought.

'However,' he said, 'we will do what we can. This bird is suffering from inflammation of the respiratory tract. I will give you some yellow powder to put in the water and you must treat them all to prevent the spread of infection. Is that clear?'

It was becoming clear to me that it was a sight easier to buy your eggs from Tesco like everybody else.

I took the yellow powder and the substantial bill, came home and treated the water. I watched my flock for improvement, but I watched in vain.

Not long after that, and I know some people will think I am making this up but I'm not, a third bird became sick. This one was gross, the worst of all. In front of her eye she developed a hard, hot, pulsating swelling. This caused the actual eyeball to foam and froth. It was truly horrible to look at. She squinted at me with a troubled air. I just could not keep a bird in that condition. The vet seemed strangely pleased to see me. 'Come in!' he gushed.

He said that, indeed, the whole flock had a viral infection and that if I wanted to I could probably take up the legal cudgels with the supplier. In the meantime he would do what he could. He gave me a phial of eye drops and a set of three pre-filled hypodermic syringes to be administered on three consecutive days. And a bill.

I don't know if you have ever tried to put eye drops in a chicken's eye but you need a steady hand and a willing chicken and I had neither. On first detecting the cold liquid in her eye she shook her head so violently that, although I had no tumescent swelling myself, I had the full benefit of the treatment. Then I had to turn her over and inject her with the syringe. I had never injected anything in my life. It was like Sunday dinner with the feathers on. It was a fiasco.

I used to have this vision. In it I wear a print dress and walk in the sunshine. Over my arm there is a basket with sweet hay nestling in the base. I step along the garden path until I reach a coop of contented chickens, clucking and fluffing up their feathers in a dust-bath. Lifting the sun-warmed lid of the nestboxes I see to my delight speckled eggs, warm and fulsome. These I place reverently into my basket. Smiling I turn and walk away, skirt billowing, until my figure is obscured and swallowed up in the hollyhocks.

The reality is harsher. The sky is grey and lowering. I am plodding across a wet field with a bucket. I am wearing my husband's Drizabone coat and the dog has chewed the hem, causing it to hang in rags. I reach the beleaguered chicken coop, there are no eggs and I didn't fancy them anyway. I fling open the door and there they are, my six chickens. One has a leg up in its feathers, it can't walk it can only hop. Another is breathing great ragged breaths, beak agape. The third is staring up at me from behind a great carbuncle. As they glare at me accusingly I hear the vet drive past in his Mercedes.

I don't keep chickens any more, although I did for a while when our children were small.

# How Can That Be My Baby?

How can that be my baby? How can that be my son?
Standing on a rugger field, more than six feet one,
Steam is rising from him, his legs are streaked with blood,
And he wears a yellow mouthguard in a face that's black
    with mud.

How can that be my baby? How can he look like that?
I used to sit him on my knee and read him *Postman Pat*,
Those little ears with cotton buds I kept in perfect shape
But now they're big and purple and they're fastened back
    with tape.

How can that be my baby? When did he reach that size?
What happened to his wellies with the little froggy eyes?
His shirt is on one shoulder but it's hanging off the other,
And the little baffled person at his feet is me:
                                             his mother.

# Thirteen-Nil

Our young son is very keen on football. After weeks of waiting and hoping, he was selected to play for the school and went off proudly in the minibus to his first match against a neighbouring school.

His father and I went to watch, along with a smattering of other parents, and found ourselves a good spot on a bank overlooking the pitch. This gave us an excellent view of our son's team as it was ignominiously beaten thirteen-nil, and a gut-wrenching look at the shading of his mood from optimism to despair. We saw the triumphant strutting of the victors and found, at the end of the match, as our son and the rest of the team walked wretchedly off the field burning with shame, that neither of us could think what to say. Words died on our lips. All around us other parents fought to find the appropriate uplifting phrase. Later, when it was not necessary to conceal my true feelings, I wrote 'Thirteen-Nil'.

# *Thirteen-Nil*

Oh the joy it was unbounded, what a thrill!
Selected for the team! I see him still,
At ten years old, what style and grace,
Those knobbly knees, that beaming face,
I felt as if *I'd* won the place ...
Thirteen-nil

Our weaknesses were speedily revealed,
The other team they swaggered round the field,
Oh my teeth I had to grit them,
If a dog had only bit them,
Our side never knew what hit them ...
Thirteen-nil

The teacher bellowed insults and abuse,
But even his support was not much use,
It was a fate so mean and cruel,
No one now was looking cool,
The laughing stock of all the school ...
Thirteen-nil

The brand-new shin protectors brought no luck,
The boy done bad: the striker never struck,
The ignominy and the shame,
To have missed the chance of fame,
And there was no one else to blame,
Thirteen-nil

It was difficult to know just what to say,
As they all trooped off the pitch at close of play,
You couldn't say, 'Whew, that was close!
You were pipped right at the post!
Why don't we all propose a toast?'
To thirteen-nil

The score to shameful jeering was announced,
Our lads defeated: absolutely trounced,
But there's one thing that's for sure,
Although the crowds they didn't roar,
Your mother loves you even more,
At thirteen-nil.

# Suet Puddings

As the mother of two sons, I always try to provide a good nutritious diet and I enjoy reading about healthy food. It's interesting to note the changes in thinking over the last forty years or so. Today we are advised to eat lots of fruit and vegetables and to reduce our intake of red meat and, more especially, of fat. This part of the message comes through most forcefully, that we should drastically cut the amount of fat in our diet.

Growing up in Stanford-in-the-Vale in the fifties, we had no inkling that fat might one day be undesirable. Indeed, fat in various forms was dished up daily with great shouts of 'This'll keep the cold out!' 'Get this across yer chest!' 'This'll warm yer, my gal!' A great smoking fry-up was looked forward to for breakfast and it came with platefuls of fried bread, golden brown and stiff with lard.

On Sunday nights we used to have slices of bread spread with dripping. Banked high, it was a rich yellow-brown, the colour of ferrets. Each bite left a great cliff face carved in fat, rather like an impression taken at the dentist's. We used to have slices of bread and lard sprinkled with sugar and I met a family not long ago who sprinkled theirs with salt, so we were able to exchange recipes.

The fat we used most was suet. It was in everything, pastry, puddings, dumplings; we were also given it to chew like chewing gum and it thickly coated the inside of your mouth. Recently I was following a recipe for some kind of casserole with dumplings and I needed to buy some suet. It was quite hard to find and I had to search along the low shelves in the supermarket where they put items not much in demand. I found it in a blue packet with a chef raising his hat and smiling ripely on the front. It was obviously good for the heart because right across the pack it said AORTA, something like that. Inside the packet was a greaseproof bag into which the suet had been extruded in uniform lengths, rather like macaroni. It seemed very sanitised indeed. My childish dealings with suet were a lot cruder.

Then Mother and I would enter the butcher's shop, paddling through a thick layer of sawdust, and approach the grey marble counter. She would ask for whatever she wanted, often shin of beef, it being cheap but very tender providing it was boiled for the full nine hours. She might then ask for a bit of suet. This was the unit in which suet was measured. Not the pound, the ounce, the kilo, but the bit. The butcher would turn and walk to the back of the shop where a line of carcasses were hung up on hooks convenient for bluebottles. He would reach inside the cavity of one of these carcasses and wrench forth a piece of suet. It used to come away with a horrible papery tearing sound that was somehow hard to forget. He would put it on the counter, wrap it up in a sheet of hygienic newspaper and hand it to Mother, who then took it home and incorporated it into a vast multitude of dishes. Some of them were savoury, like the Bacon Clanger, but for the most part they were sweet.

Bread pudding was one of the great favourites, at least it was the great favourite of our mother. We kids hated the stuff, but it was heartily approved of by our parents because it used something which would otherwise have gone to waste. In that post-war period waste was understandably regarded with outrage. Some evenings we would all sit round the fire having sandwiches. If one of us couldn't quite manage the last crust, and there was a good blaze going in the grate, he might have felt his trigger finger itching to flick the crust into the fire. No chance. Father had a sort of sixth sense of what you might be planning to do and his voice would boom out like the voice of doom: 'BURN BREAD – LIVE TO WANT!' The trigger finger would wilt and die.

Any such fragments of bread were normally gathered up by Mother and all crusts, ends of loaves, and so on, were placed to soak, in a galvanised bucket of water kept covered by the pastry board, on the floor of the larder. When they were sufficiently steeped, she would stagger in with the bucket and wring out the bread on the kitchen table. The wet mass went into a gigantic mixing bowl, and even the water in which the bread had lain was not wasted, for it was shipped off to a neighbour who had a pig. The pig's owner worked for the railways and had constructed a pigsty entirely out of railway sleepers. This was a robust pigsty which could have contained a moderately active rhinoceros. The pig, peering out through meagre cracks between the tar-soaked sleepers, developed a startling black-striped face, not unlike a zebra.

Back in the kitchen mother was transforming the wet bread into bread pudding: adding two spoonfuls of mixed spice, grating in the suet and counting in the currants. The whole treacly-sounding mixture was then churned into what the cookbooks described as A Dropping Consistency. This was then Dropped into a large, blackened meat-roasting tin, pressed well down and put into the oven to bake. I don't remember how long it was baked for, but certainly it was until all the little currants sticking out of the top had turned to coal. Mother would carve it into giant cubes and it would be served with custard. It had a very dense texture. If you held it up to the light you couldn't see any air holes in it. It was interesting because once you had eaten it you never had to ask yourself, 'Have I been fed, or not?' because it sat there like a brick. You could feel your gastric juices trying to get the better of it.

In addition to bread pudding, we had the more traditional type of suet pudding, which came in the shape of a great sagging sausage, or bomb. I used to watch Mum make it, see it patted, floured and wrapped up in a piece of sheet salvaged from a sheet which had gone in the middle. She used to tie it up at each end so it couldn't make a dash for it, then lower it into a big black saucepan on the kitchen range. It would be brought up to a good rolling boil and then she would go off and get on with whatever else she had to do. The thing boiled all day, boiled and rolled until the windows downstairs, upstairs and next door were all steamed up and pouring with condensation. At the end of the day everyone would come home. My dad would come from the Electricity Board, my four brothers from their various trades and my sister from school. We would all sit at the table and wait to be fed. We ate a lot of rabbit then, all the country people did; this was before myxomatosis struck, nobody ate rabbit after that. Dad used to catch them, he would come home at night swathed in rabbits and heave them onto the draining board. Mother's face would drop because she would have to think of new and innovative ways to serve them. We had roast rabbit, rabbit stew, rabbit fricassee, rabbit in the hole. I always thought that had a kind of lunatic logic to it.

When we finished the main course, Mum would get the pudding. She would fish it out of the saucepan, lower it on to the big oval platter and whip off the cloth, matador fashion. There it would lie, this great smoking suet duff. You could always tell when it was done because it used to turn an attractive shiny grey colour. Mum would slice it up and serve it, and it was named according to the filling it contained, so that if it had dates or currants in, it was a traditional Spotted Dick, if it had home-made jam rolled up inside it, that was a Jam Roly-Poly, if it contained apples and cloves, we used to call that an Apple Duff, and if it had no filling at all, if Mum couldn't afford anything and it was just plain, we used to call it Old Lady's Leg. You had it with custard or Golden Syrup, and it was very beneficial to the arteries. There were regional variations of that name: in a neighbouring village they called it Drowned Sailor's Arm.

My mother had great faith in the restorative properties of the suet pudding. Dad was part of what they called the Shut-down Gang, and it was this gang which was called out if the electricity supply had been interrupted and areas were without power. People used to come for Dad late on stormy nights and he would go out, all wrapped up, holding the great spikes they strapped to their legs to enable them to walk up poles. I found it highly dramatic. Dad would come back sometime the next day, utterly exhausted, often drenched through. He would stand framed in the door and say, 'I be soaked'. If it was hot he would be parched dry, covered in a fine film of road dust. Then he would say, 'I be choked.' So you did get a certain amount of seasonal variation.

Mother's response was always the same. She would go over to him and say, 'You come on in here, Stan. What you need is a bowl of pudding!' She would lay a place for him on our little gate-leg table and go off to get some. It was always very stylishly served, in a white pudding basin with a spoon stuck vertically in the top, and it was always murderously hot. If it was not lethally hot, it wasn't ready. It came in like a train by night, with a plume of steam travelling behind it. Mum would put it down in front of him and go off, leaving it to work its magic. Father would shape up to it like a prize fighter, pushing up his sleeves, and when he first sat down the column of steam rising from it was so profuse that it would engulf his head as he leaned forward to eat it. You could see his arm going up and down but you couldn't see his actual face. Eventually the steam would clear and then you could see him in there. His face would be a bright boiling red, with trickles of sweat running down his temples and dripping off his chin. He had a wonderful sense of humour. He used to catch my eye and say, 'Phew. I'll be glad when I've had enough.'

# The Biological Clock

I did not go through my early life longing to start a family. I loved writing and performing and was intrigued to see where they might take me.

When I found I was expecting a baby I was excited, but unprepared for the might of the maternal instinct. After he was born, I found that when I was away from my son, I developed a real, aching pain in my chest which disappeared as soon as we were reunited. He was like an extension of myself, an arm, a shoulder, something from which it was unimaginable to be parted. All the work seemed unimportant, a poor, limping second.

I would never have believed I could change so much.

This new mum is also plunged into a world of changed priorities. She finds that leaving her baby with a nanny is not as straightforward as she thought.

# *The Biological Clock*

## A Song

I used to make executive decisions,
My hand was the hand at the controls,
Now I sit at home with little babies
Posting plastic shapes into the holes,

It's the clock, the clock,
The biological clock,

The clock that made me think it's now or never
To have a baby now or not at all,
Now I think that when I heard it ticking
Perhaps I should have thrown it at the wall.

I used to like the challenge of the boardroom,
I used to like the playful cut and thrust,
But ever since I had a little baby,
My faculties are seizing up with rust.
I used to sit on every committee,
My opinions dispelling any doubt,
Now at Nursery I see the other mothers,
But I don't know what to talk to them about.

But you should have seen me coping with a crisis,
You should have seen me brokering a deal,
But now I'm in the market for a nanny,
And I think I'm going to need my nerves of steel.
She wants a flat. I gave her that.
I can hear her music halfway up the street
She wants a car, well, there you are,
And here's a list of what she wants to eat.

But it's strange now I'm back in full employment,
Back where I can make a hostile bid,
That I seem to lack a little concentration
And the work seems less important than it did.
The motivation of the team has lost its glitter,
The new incentive scheme has lost its charms,
There's been a certain downturn in the market
And I want to feel my baby in my arms.

He's got no teeth! He's got no hair,
But I sit at work and don't want to be there,
It's not my choice, what can I do?
I just prefer him to a VDU.
I'm going home, I'm going back,
And I'm going to greet the nanny with the sack,
In business terms, I was a rock,
But I didn't have the strength to beat the clock,

The clock, the clock,
The biological clock,
Tick-tock, it's the clock,
The biological clock.

# Barbecues

I am not a very good cook. I have tried over the years, but I get too tense, clutch the recipe book too tightly, pore too worriedly over the detail. I have no natural flair. Early in my married life I used to try to have smart little dinners and they were like a scene out of Dr Jekyll and Mr Hyde, with me beaming at the expectant guests then, in the miserable solitude of the kitchen, leaping from one leg to the other, not knowing what to do first. I've got friends who are not fazed by the arrival of a dozen hungry and unexpected guests: they place a large pan, smilingly, on the hob, flinging in this and that while filling people's glasses and laughing with bright-eyed merriment. I am not one of those lucky people. I can only watch that sort of person with incredulity and sharp envy.

This is why I like barbecues.

A barbecue seems to me to be the antidote to all that. A barbecue is enjoyed out in the open air, and the burden of responsibility does not fall on the shoulders of one sweat-drenched woman toiling alone in the kitchen, but is enjoyably shared among the many. A barbecue does not involve forcing reluctant children to sit up properly at a table and not fiddle. They can rush off and play. At the end of a barbecue no mountain of good china waits to be washed, no quality glasses wait to be patted dry, no best tablecloth sneers from under stains of wine and blobs of thick sauce. After a barbecue most of what remains can be heaved into a bin liner or fed to the dog.

The finest one I ever went to was in Vancouver in Canada. A vet friend of my husband invited us to his home. A fellow guest had been fishing that day and had caught a large, plump salmon from one of the heart-stoppingly beautiful rivers in British Columbia. The fish was lightly marinaded then barbecued in the back garden. All around were conifers giving off a thick and intoxicating smell of pine. The memory of those kind people, the magical setting and that exquisite fish is as vivid to me now as it was twenty years ago.

Last year we were invited several times to barbecues at the home of one of our friends. They were lovely evenings. My friend has a paved terrace with a pergola. Climbing up and over it are stunning clematis and a magnificent rose in the palest pearly pink, not one of those roses where one bloom comes out and everybody celebrates, but a generous and abundant rose, a rose bent double with blooms, clustered and plastered and falling over itself with gushing roses. Petals tumbled down beside me as I sat with a glass of hock. The wine not the horse's back leg. My friend would put out bowls of cut-up buttered French sticks, masses of colourful salad and pressed-glass dishes of little sweet tomatoes. Her husband was an Ace Barbecuer who took it very seriously. He wore a long, spotless white apron and a big hat. From time to time he would extend a languid hand for things unfamiliar to me: balsamic vinegar, juniper berries and a giant pepper mill like the leg of the bed. She, wisely, left him to get on with it.

We loved going there but after a period it was clear that an imbalance was being created, the invitations were one-sided, and, as my husband gravely said, 'If you go, you owe.'

I suggested to him that we had room for a barbecue ourselves. I pointed out the various nooks and crannies where one could be inconspicuously tucked and added that our boys in their early teens could only benefit. Young friends could come round. We could have sausage sizzles in the sunshine. My husband agreed.

'Yes,' he said sagely, 'yes. And I will build it.'

I felt a certain sinking of the heart.

He went to Travis Perkins for some leaflets and over a few cold weekends built us a barbecue in the garden. I was excited. It looked like the real thing. As soon as the first decent day came, I was on the phone. 'Come on!' I urged my family and friends. 'Drop what you're doing! We're having our first barbecue! It's finished and we're giving it a go! The wine's in the fridge, get round here!' Even my two frail aunties, sisters well into their eighties who venture out only rarely, agreed to come.

It was not a success.

Afterwards I did what I should have done in the first place, which was to study the design of my friend's efficient barbecue. I noted that it had three levels. The first one was a tray on which you placed the fuel. The next was a sturdy cooking rack which could be fitted in any of three positions according to how close to the heat source you wanted the food to be. The third was a natty half-shelf, just above and set back from the cooking rack, where the food could be rested until you were ready for it.

Ours was different. Ours was a simpler design. It had only two main features: the lower tray for fuel and an upper rack for cooking on, the position of which could not be adjusted. On the fateful first night it soon became clear that all was not well. The food cooked too fast. My husband fuelled it with lumpwood charcoal which burned at such a furnace-like pitch that when he approached it he had to shield his face from the blistering heat. He flung the meat on to the grid from two paces away while looking backwards. It cleaved to the white-hot metal, shrank and blackened before his bloodshot eyes. For their supper people were given sagging paper plates bearing knobs of a hard black material. These might as well have been lifted straight out of the coal scuttle. My two aunties, far from receiving what two frail and elderly persons might reasonably expect, namely some small and tantalising morsel served with due regard to colour and appetising appearance, were given a pile of blackened shapes. They studied them, mystified. I heard one say, 'I don't think I can manage it dear. He said it was a chop.' I did see her attack it timidly with tremulous gums, give up and drop it furtively behind the viburnum.

My feelings on the subject of barbecues are jaded now and summed up quite successfully in 'Won't Someone Take Our Barbecue Away?'

# Won't Someone Take Our Barbecue Away?

## A Song

Won't someone take our barbecue away?
Father thinks about it night and day,
Oh he's lining it with foil,
And he's brushing it with oil,
From now until the spring,
There's just one thing
I want to say:

We're having no more barbecues round here,
We're going to permit the smoke to clear,
No more sausages to char,
No more coming as you are,
As your shish kebab gets crisper,
Let me whisper
In your ear:

The final greasy chin is paper-towelled,
The final chipolata disembowelled,
No more standing in the queue,
No more leather left to chew,
No more bring a bottle,
Though I don't know what
He'll do.

It's just a simple structure made of brick,
But it seemed to get a hold of him so quick,
In his apron and his thongs,
With his bloodshot eyes and tongs,
It's like the gates of Hell,
I hate the smell,
It makes me sick.

But to his tragic fate we are resigned,
The poor old devil's barbecued his mind,
Now he's dancing in the heat,
'Cause the coals fell on his feet,
Oh take away his fuel,
Let's be cruel
To be kind.

As long as he's got charcoal on the grate,
We know that we'll have charcoal … on the plate,
Oh the duck he cooked was black,
But the inside still went 'Quack!'
If you're after salmonella, he's your fella,
He's your mate.

He used to be an ordinary bloke,
Until he found excitement up the smoke,
Now it's plates of runny butter,
It's the black hole of Calcutta,
Beside the flaming grill,
We will trill,
Our sweet refrain.

Even now he's out there in the snow,
Still trying to get the bloody thing to go,
Oh he's piling up the coal,
And he's blowing in the hole,
I hate to break it to you
But it's true,
You have to know ...

We're having no more barbecues round here,
It's time to wash and pack away the gear,
As the sun goes down and sets
Take your charcoal and briquettes,
For one thing I'm assuring you my dear,
We're having no more barbecues
    round here.

# *Yes, I'll Marry You,*
## *My Dear*

Yes, I'll marry you, my dear, and here's the reason why:
So I can push you out of bed when the baby starts
   to cry,
And if we hear a knocking and it's creepy and it's late,
I hand you the torch you see and *you* investigate.

Yes, I'll marry you, my dear, you may not apprehend it,
But when the tumble-drier goes it's you that has to mend it,
You have to face the neighbour, should our Labrador
   attack him,
And if a drunkard fondles me, it's you that has to
   whack him.

Yes, I'll marry you, my dear, you're virile and you're
     lean,
My house is like a pigsty, you can help to keep it clean,
That little sexy dinner which you served by candlelight,
As I just do chipolatas, you can cook it every night!

It's you who has to work the drill and put up curtain
     track,
And when I've got the PMT it's you who gets the flak,
I do see great advantages, but none of them for you,
And so before you see the light, I do I do I do!

# Ivy on the Bricks

## A Song

Down along this railway line we used to take a stroll,
You would bring a bucket, love, and pick up lumps of coal,
Underneath this very bridge we held a crucifix
And swore our love was true, but now there's ivy on
    the bricks.

Ivy on the bricks me gal, ivy on the bricks,
Nothing lasts for ever and there's ivy on the bricks.

On the final night beneath the bridge without a care,
I took you in my arms and you had ivy in your hair,
Alas we never saw the fast-approaching 8:06
And when the train had vanished there was ivy on
    the bricks,

Ivy on the bricks me gal, ivy on the bricks,
All my hopes were flattened, there was ivy on the bricks.

I built a mausoleum and erected it to you,
With cherabim and seraphim, it cost a bob or two,
Up on the inscription our initials intermix,
But take your secateurs because there's ivy on the bricks.

Ivy on the bricks me gal, ivy on the bricks,
For nothing lasts for ever and there's ivy on the bricks.

# When Will I Have Suffered Enough?

When will I have suffered enough?
When will I have suffered enough?
I bathed him and fed him and coaxed up each burp,
I bought him revolvers just like Wyatt Earp,
And now I must welcome his wife, who's a twerp.
When will I have suffered enough?

# Saint Tesco

One day I was walking my dog beyond Cherry Tree Lane, a spot where you need a fertile imagination as it isn't a lane and there aren't any cherry trees. There is however a pleasant unfolding view of the town of Cirencester. It was at about eleven o'clock on a Sunday morning shortly after legislation had been passed to permit the Sunday opening of supermarkets.

On the far side of the town I could see the handsome perpendicular tower of the church of St John the Baptist, ancient, imposing and reputed to be larger than three of England's cathedrals. In the foreground I could see a much less historic feature of the town, the new Tesco supermarket. This too had a tower, with Tesco on it in red writing. I stood for a moment and gazed at the vast expanse of slate-grey roof, then looked across and up at the tower of the church. I did this a few times, rather like a person watching Wimbledon. From my vantage point I could see that the supermarket was a bustle of activity. Fleets of cars followed one another into the car park and toiled out nose-to-tail at the opposite end. People with bags and trolleys and children criss-crossed the scene, security guards glowered, keen lads threw themselves into the task of pushing ninety-five trolleys all locked together and the whole scene was brisk and purposeful.

Although I couldn't see the area around the church at that time, I imagined it to be somewhat different. I had often passed through the Market Place on a Sunday morning, and knew there would be various knots of people waiting to go into church for the service. They would be smartly dressed, predominantly of an older generation, gathered into little groups of friends and family. Something about the scene always left me with a sense of melancholy, of bewilderment that the Church and religion, that very faith which caused these mighty buildings to be created, could dwindle to such an extent that these one or two beleaguered groups gathered on the pavement could be all that was left, all that remained on the sand as the tide of belief receded away after centuries.

That Sunday morning observation of the church tower and the newly built supermarket gave me the idea for 'Nowadays We Worship at Saint Tesco'.

# Nowadays We Worship at Saint Tesco

Nowadays we worship at Saint Tesco,
At first the neighbours seemed a little shocked,
But then, Saint Tesco's doors are always open,
Whereas Saint Cuthbert's doors are always locked.
It's hard to get to know the congregation,
And the vicar isn't actually ordained,
They haven't got a pulpit or a chancel,
But they've got enormous windows: and they're
    stained.

I'm glad we're in the parish of Saint Tesco,
I feel so happy walking down the aisle,
The Reverend was always rather gloomy,
But the check-out girls have always got a smile,
Their uniform is anything but dreary,
It's polyester cotton and it's striped,
Pretty tunes come floating down from Heaven
It isn't organ music: but it's piped.

Thank Heavens I converted to Saint Tesco,
I find this new religion suits me fine,
It's altogether younger than Saint Cuthbert's
Where the congregation all look ninety-nine,
The vicar used to talk about the prophets,
But he didn't mean the same as you and I,
He couldn't hold a candle to Saint Tesco,
And anyway, his steeple's not so high.

Sometimes I dream I'm sitting in Saint Cuthbert's,
In that old pew where water always dripped,
I can smell the incense sweetly burning,
And the rising damp that flourished in the crypt,
Today no candles twinkle at the window
And no confetti lingers round the gate,
No more blushing brides and bouncing babies,
Verily. It's passed its sell-by date.

But business is booming at Saint Tesco,
The worshippers are spending more and more,
They're getting such a throng on Sunday morning,
That they're going to have to reinforce the floor,
Frankly, it has been a revelation,
On Sundays now we relish going out,
And seeing all that inexpensive lager
Has made my husband so much more devout.

They're stripping out the timber at Saint Cuthbert's,
It doesn't earn enough to pay its keep,
They ought to take a lesson from Saint Tesco
And learn to pile it high and sell it cheap,
Some ladies still are singing in the choir,
Of the Earth they will inherit if they're meek,
But Saint Tesco have on high the voice of angels,
With all the special offers for the week!

Yet sometimes in the busy supermarket,
Above the merry ringing of the till,
I fancy I can hear a church bell ringing
From the steeple of Saint Cuthbert's on the hill,
The bell has gone, the roof, the stained-glass window,
I daresay it's a merciful release,
For nowadays we worship at Saint Tesco,
It's closing time Saint Cuthbert:

                                        Rest in peace.

# The National Lottery

When the new National Lottery was launched I enjoyed a sense of happy anticipation. I rushed to buy my tickets in the hope that it would be a force for good, with fabulous riches for the lucky few and national projects on a grand scale for the good of all.

I was crestfallen, then, to note the reaction of the first few lucky winners and the speed with which they became the subject of litigation. Each one, it seemed, was being sued by an aggrieved partner for a wad of the cash. The mother of one was quoted in the newspaper as saying, 'I hope he drinks himself to death,' a sentiment of goodwill if ever there was one. A young man who had lived with a woman for a period of years announced, when she wanted a share of his winnings, 'Yes, I have lived with her for years but she was only an acquaintance.'

I have had to conclude that big lottery wins may not necessarily bring out the most unselfish traits in the human being. People, and of course I include myself, do not buy a lottery ticket and hope that someone else wins. These thoughts gave me the idea for my lottery poem 'Let It Be Me'.

# Let It Be Me

I want to win the National Lottery,
I won't be mean, I'll give to charity,
So let me flee this life of stress,
Slowly rise and whisper, 'Yes!'
Send the money by express!
Let it be me

I beg you Mr Camelot and Co.,
There's things about my life you just can't know
We were poor beyond compare;
All our cupboards, they were bare,
I'm just asking you: be fair!
Let it be me

I know some poor folks' lives are filled with knocks,
I know some poor folks' homes' a cardboard box,
I wish them mansions, food and wine,
All six numbers in a line,
As soon as I've collected mine,
Let it be me

I could walk away from work and I'd be free
The interest rate would hold no fear for me,
I could go to France and Rome,
The Greek Islands I could comb,
And my wife could stay at home,
Let it be me

Gambling my friends? I've tried it all,
I never had the luck, no luck at all,
I never held the winning card,
Ernie never coughed: it's hard,
The road to riches locked and barred,
Let it be me

Everybody wants to win it's true,
It's just that I deserve it more than you,
So let the joy transform my face,
Let my balls drop into place,
Out of all the human race:
Let it be me!

# Close Together: Far Apart

## A Song

We live close together and so far apart,
Joy in our faces and grief in our heart,
There's no common ground left between us at all,
But we love our children,
They're helpless and small.

Who'd have foreseen it would turn out this way,
No lover, no friend at the end of the day,
Must we be joined in a battle of wills,
Who pays the mortgage
And who pays the bills?

Who gets the custody, who will it be,
Who gets the holidays, you or me?
When can they come and how soon must they leave,
Who gets the birthday,
Who gets Christmas Eve?

Who runs to comfort the cry in the dark,
Who gets weekends and the walk in the park?
It's business as usual, divorce is no shame,
Oh, but where will I be
When they're calling my name ...

# The Ski-ing Plumber

There goes the ski-ing plumber,
There goes the ski-ing plumber,
His pace has never flagged,
All in his padded clothing,
By Golly, he's well lagged.

# History of Littering

One hot day, I was waiting in a queue of traffic, in my car, at a place called Preston Toll Bar, near my home. This is a road junction where a smaller country road joins a thundering bypass and is one of my most hated places. It terrifies me.

The cars, including mine, were lined up next to the small village green on the edge of Preston village. There is a notice board and a full, beautiful horse chestnut tree. Someone had gone to the trouble of mowing the little green and it looked very sweet and wholesome. I was looking fondly at it when the driver of the stationary car in front of me wound down his window and heaved out onto the grass a great fistful of litter. It blew across the little green, the crisp packets, the fag ends, the silver paper. Of course I should have marched smartly up, banged on the window and remonstrated with him, pricked his conscience, appealed to his better nature. On the other hand he might have hit me with a pickaxe handle. So I fumed in my car, fumed all the way home, where I then sat down and started to write this poem called 'Littering'.

# Littering

I love to go driving around in my car,
Visiting beauty spots near and afar,
They're pretty of course and attractive indeed,
But always I sense a continuing need:
They want littering,
Littering,
There, where the songbirds are twittering
A plastic bag, tattered and blowing in strips,
One or two boxes of curry and chips,
The very idea has me smacking my lips
To go littering.

Along the canal I go walking each day,
I think of the navvies who puddled the clay,
It's calm and serene and we owe them so much,
But still it is lacking that finishing touch,
It needs littering,
Littering,
There, where the water is glittering,
Nothing too drastic, a touch here and there,
A half-submerged mattress, an old swivel chair,
A Sainsbury's trolley stuck up in the air
Going littering.

My girlfriend and I, we get weary of town,
So we park in the woods with our windows wound
  down,
We breathe the sweet air: no pollution, no smoke,
And toss from the window our old cans of Coke,
We go littering,
Littering,
And that sets my girlfriend off tittering,
Then in the fondest embraces we lock,
Out on the grass go her knickers, her frock,
And items that might give your granny a shock,
We're just littering.

I love to visit the stateliest homes,
To wander amid the cupolas and domes,
I take a nice picnic, a mug and a flask,
And then, when I've finished, I go ... need you ask?
I go littering,
Littering,
Down where the mayflies are skittering,
Next to the river I wander about,
Throwing in fag ends to nourish the trout,
And doing my bit to assist in the drought,
I go littering.

Often I amble down some leafy street,
Admiring the lawns and the gardens so neat,
The shrubs and the borders, the ferns and the ponds
And yet in the shadow there, under the fronds ...
It needs littering,
Littering,
There where the butterfly's flittering,
So over your wall, and by golly I'm quick,
Go old paper tissues, a bottle, a brick,
Or sometimes I'll just lean across and be sick,
It's all littering.

I love to spread litter wherever I go,
I cast it about me like manna, like snow,
I give to the woods and the path and the lake
That dollop of icing on top of the cake,
I go littering,
Littering,
My footsteps come patter and pittering,
Disposable nappies, a glorious sight
All bundled up, sort of yellow and white,
For I have a true, unassailable right
To go littering.

I'm off to the country to stand and to stare,
To take all my junk and abandon it there,
Driving my van up the old railway track,
I'll heave kitchen units from out of the back,
I'm just littering,
Littering,
I haven't the time to waste frittering,
I've fridges and freezers, a washing machine,
An old iron bedstead once graced by the Queen,
If you're looking for something that changes the scene
You need littering.

Where bridges cross rivers I stand on the span,
Dropping in rings from the top of a can,
Where wind stirs the grass of a field or a verge,
I feel this compulsion: this primitive urge,
To go littering,
Littering,
When so much in this world is embittering,
The job satisfaction is pure and divine,
This plastic will be here ten years down the line
And like silver paper my efforts will shine,
I went littering.

# *If Only Once Again My Hair Would Sprout*

If only once again my hair would sprout,
If what came up matched what was falling out,
If I could rub the Silvikrin,
On something more than skin,
Then with exhilaration I would shout.

Once I had a fine abundant shock,
When vigour palpitated down each lock,
And barbers were in tears,
In the search to find my ears,
And where I found a long-lost shuttlecock.

I was the man extravagantly maned,
Sculpted and meticulously trained,
Luxuriant and plush,
Like a lavatory brush,
Similar to *Hercules Unchained*.

In the local cinema it's true,
My hair in all its splendour blocked the view,
Picturegoers used to rant,
As they searched for Cary Grant,
And outside it kept the drizzle off the queue.

Wigmakers salivated as I passed,
But now before the mirror, I'm aghast,
I offer free to loving home,
One redundant brush and comb,
My friends *Adieu!* Take this shampoo. It was my last.

My noble central parting, plain and clear,
Is now located just above my ear,
And a single lonely tress,
Has to hide my nakedness,
Not easy when it's breezy from the rear.

I remember when the women were enthralled,
They have vanished now my name is being called,
Resistance it is fruitless,
For I am summoned rootless,
To the regions, to the legions of the bald.

# In the Merc

## The Tycoon's Song

When I drove a Ford my heart was always far away,
In a Merc, in a Merc,
I fantasised in Vauxhalls or astride a BSA
Of a Merc, of a Merc,
And to myself I swore you would discover me one day
In a Merc, in a Merc, in a Merc.

Now I drive at ninety miles an hour along the motorway,
In my Merc, in my Merc,
But the hair that flies behind me is a whiter shade of grey,
In the Merc, in the Merc,
And all the pretty girls, they turn and look the other way,
In the Merc, in the Merc, in the Merc.

See me in the street I drive with confidence and verve,
In the Merc, in the Merc,
The seats are creamy leather and I love their every curve,
In the Merc, in the Merc,
But now they just play havoc with my trapped sciatic nerve,
In the Merc, in the Merc, in the Merc.

I open up the top and I feel vibrant and alive,
In the Merc, in the Merc,
But bees bounce off the glasses that I have to wear to drive,
In the Merc, in the Merc,
And I think I pulled more birds when I was in a Renault 5,
Than the Merc, than the Merc, than the Merc.

This poem was much influenced by the Michael Flanders and
Donald Swann song 'In the Bath'.

# The Wonderbra

I bought myself one of those books that tell you how to develop your own style, how to buy the few key items of clothing that enable you to have, ready at hand, the perfect outfit for any occasion. This was an attractive notion to me as I have ninety-nine items in my wardrobe, none of which go together.

On reading the book it was clear that the first task was to identify your own body shape from a selection of diagrams. Having looked at them all, I concluded that I was Pear Shaped With a Short Neck. This was not necessarily the description I would have chosen for myself, but there was no argument, this was the shape which most resembled mine.

Next came advice on what to wear for those who were Pear Shaped With a Short Neck. Avoid high necks, it said, as they foreshorten the already shortened neck. Opt instead for V-necks, revere collars and similar shapes because these, it said, favourably elongate the throat. This seemed sensible advice and anyway my husband has often said he would like to elongate my throat.

Christmas was coming and I was in need of a new dress, so I took into account the helpful words in my book and bought a very chic black dress with a deep V-neck. It was a change, I could wear a glitzy necklace, and I liked it. Never having had such a neckline before, however, I overlooked what many women have overlooked before me. The right underwear. To my disappointment at home I found that not one bra of my current collection was suitable, all of them thrust themselves tart-like into the smart neckline. I went back to the shops to buy a new one.

At this time there was an advertising campaign running for the Wonderbra. It was everywhere you looked, on hoardings, in favourite magazines. It featured a voluptuous bra-clad model entering a room uttering provocative statements like 'Size does matter!' and 'Hello, boys!' with the promise in her eyes of good things to come. It had the desired effect because I bought one myself. In Bournemouth.

At home that night I put it on. There wasn't much to it really, thin straps, a couple of scalloped edges and two little dolly's pillows of white padding. Anyway, it was a good fit. It was fine. Well, it was fine as long as I was standing up straight, BUT when I leaned forward to feed the cat, the whole operation felt rather less than secure. I persevered with it for a bit, but in the end I gave up and took it back to the shop. I bought something rather more robust, something that felt more like me. Not, however, before the Wonderbra gave me the idea for this little song.

# The Wonderbra Song

I bought myself a Wonderbra
   for fourteen ninety-nine,
It looked so good on the model girl's chest,
   and I hoped it would on mine,
I took it from the packaging
   and when I tried it on,
The Wonderbra restored to me
   all I believed had gone ...

*Chorus*:

Let's all salute the Wonderbra,
   the Wonderbra, the Wonderbra,
Let's all salute the Wonderbra,
   for fourteen ninety-nine.

It gave me such a figure,
    I can't believe it's mine,
I showed it to my husband
    and it made his eyeballs shine,
And when I served the breakfast,
    the kids cried out, 'Hooray!
Here comes our darling mother,
    with her bosom on a tray!'

I didn't really need one,
    my present bra, it's true,
Had only been in constant use
    since nineteen eighty-two,
But the silhouette I dreamed about,
    is mine, is mine at last,
And builders on the scaffolding,
    drop off as I walk past ...

*Chorus*:

Singing ... let's all salute the Wonderbra,
    the Wonderbra, the Wonderbra,
Let's all salute the Wonderbra
    For fourteen ninety-nine!

# Popocatepetl

Our school seemed to be spread all over the town. There was a bit made out of old army huts where we did needlework. You had to walk across the railway line and past the old sawmill for that. Then there was a bunch of Nissen huts where we did maths and art, filthy tarry old buildings. Yobs used to break in and leave ... items on the floor. Then there was the school building itself, painted cream and green. I couldn't vouch for the educational standards but, my, you got plenty of exercise. When it rained you got wet legs too. When I think of that school I remember having wet muddy legs from trekking about and I remember the smell of cheap wet shoe leather.

Roneo'd sheets played a big part in our education before Mrs Pearce came on the scene. The teacher came round with printed sheets bearing information for you to learn. The trouble was that duplication was at a fairly early stage then and involved much cranking of the handle of an inky old Gestetner. A lot of the sheets didn't come out too well and missing bits had to be hurriedly drawn in later by hand. The sorts of thing they handed out were maps with dots or sausage shapes drawn on them. These represented cities or ports or ranges of hills and you had to write in the name. I remember one of Wales where you had to fill in the sort of coal mined in a particular area. Anthracite was one. Yes, well, it was dull. I hated geography. History I did not much like either, except that I was quite good at drawing horses, so I spent a lot of time drawing variations on Women in Tudor Dress on Horseback. It's funny really, looking back. All that stuff I fought to remember, the glaciated valleys, the stratification of the soil, the boring old fossils. It was as dry as chaff when I got it and forty years on it's dry as chaff still.

Well, it all comes down to the teaching of course. When Mrs Pearce came on the scene it was some time before I realised what we'd got. You see, she wasn't much to look at. She chain-smoked for a start and had breath like the fiery furnace. If ever you had to go to the staffroom because somebody had fallen over or had started their periods, well you just knew she would come squinting to the door with a fag hanging out of her mouth. She had a really haphazard hairstyle, dark brown and boringly shaped with plenty of ratty bits. She had little brown eyes that were so bright and quick. I can't remember her clothes, but they were pretty dull. She had a terrible thick cough too, which I never thought much about at the time.

But it was when she talked. You didn't care what she looked like then, whether her hair was roughed up or she was wearing her laughable old Roman Gladiator sandals. She could talk to you and the boring old cream and green room and your wet legs just faded away. She never bothered with roneo'd sheets. She'd have laughed, that sinister chesty laugh with her head thrown back. I learned more from her in the short time she was there than I did in the rest of the lessons put together.

She had travelled, you see. Not like now when, no matter where you go, you see people swigging Coke and watching the same TV programmes. I'll tell you something she did. She told us about Innsbruck in Austria. She said one night she came out of the hotel and looked up. She saw a light in the sky. She thought it was a plane except that it stood still. She looked and looked, and so did we, and as she looked she suddenly realised that the light was coming not from a plane, or from a star, but from a *home* and she realised with a shock of amazement that somebody lived up there, right up there on the side of the mountain, and she put her hand over her mouth as it dawned on her, and so did we because we could see it too and we were amazed.

She'd been to Mexico and seen the volcano Popocatepetl. We all said it together Pop-o-cat-e-petl. She'd been to Ecuador and seen another volcano Cotopaxi. Co-to-pax-i. She'd seen the active volcano called Mount Batur in Bali. She fired us up. All we knew of volcanos was that molten lava shot out of them somehow and you could buy a cheap firework of the same name. But when she described Mount Batur, she made us shudder. She said the fire did not shoot out of it. She said a column of smoke just rose out of it. One plume so you knew it was in there. And though all round the base of the volcano was green and thick and luxuriant, all running down from the rim was black and dead and sulphurous. We could see it. She told us about the beggar children who had run up to her with baskets of carvings, only they were made of bone, white bleached bone. We looked at each other in thrills of horror. Bones of *what*? She said the bone carvings chattered together in the basket as they ran. And as she sat on the desk in her flappy old sandals it was no exaggeration to say that scenes rose up behind her, rugged jungles and parched deserts and fear and thrills. It was as though I was studying geography for the first time. I had walked across a confetti of roneo'd sheets to get to the real thing.

I truly loved her. I did. Her lessons were like magic. They had the power to transport you and I worked like a dog to win her approval.

Anyway one day she set us some homework.

'I want a picture,' she said, 'a picture of somewhere in the world you'd like to visit and half a page saying why.'

That was it, the gladiator sandals were uncrossed, she sprang down from the desk and scurried off with her purposeful, inelegant walk to the staffroom and, no doubt, the tenth fag of the day

Of course I did Popocatepetl. I mean the closest I'd come to Mexico was *The Cisco Kid* on TV, and his crony Pancho who wore a ten-gallon hat, but that didn't deter me. With my mother's giant pastry board across my lap in the chair by the kitchen fire I set to with pencils and cheap paints to capture the essence of old Mexico. I had a rolling desert in the foreground, dunes reaching away into the distance: Lawrence of Arabia would have felt at home. I had the scene studded with whiskery cacti and baked by the pitiless sun I'd read about in my brother's cowboy books. I had a Mexican on a donkey crossing the sand and I made the donkey's head hang down as if it was half dead with thirst. All the practice I'd had with Ladies in Tudor Dress on Horseback stood me in good stead there and I felt the detail in the foreground was quite good. Then, holding my breath, across the great white space I'd left for the sky, I sketched in the awesome shape of Popocatepetl. It soared up into the heights, its shoulders creased and crinkled with purple shadow. At the top it had no point or peak. Having never seen the thing I gave my imagination free reign. I chopped the top straight across. Dribbling and rolling down from the rim came thick lava, black with red cracks. Firing up into the atmosphere went great bolts of molten rock, white-hot boulders and boiling black balls of smoke. I could hear the deep terrifying booms and cracks. Shudders radiated out from it and I felt them pass beneath my feet. Heat came scorching across the miles at me and the skin of my face was baked and dry like paper.

'Want a jam tart?' Mother had proffered the plate.

Anyway I was delighted with it. I put it into my satchel reverently, without folding it anywhere, and I could not wait to give it to Mrs Pearce the next day. She would know about the feelings I had when I did it, she would read what the picture meant to me.

Next day we were all in the form room waiting for geography and I was ready to burst with pride. She was a long time coming and I started to get a feeling I didn't much like. I could tell by the way the door opened that it wasn't her. She had a way of punching it open.

It was Jock Lewis, who used to take us before. He came in, cleared his throat and waited for silence.

'4B, good morning,' he began. 'Mrs Pearce is unfortunately unwell so I shall be taking you for geography.'

I just hated that, you know, so vague and open-ended. When was she coming back? When could I give her the picture? Do you know, I remember that day. It was as though someone turned the lights out.

One day about a week afterwards she still hadn't come back and we had needlework. We set off in a long crocodile to the old army huts I told you about. Two by two, along the edge of the allotments, down over the railway line, in through the gates past the derelict guardroom. I found myself walking alongside the teacher. She was young and taken up with herself. I was desperate for news. I knew I was no favourite of this teacher, but I still asked in my clumsy way,

'Miss, where's Mrs Pearce?'

'She's ill,' came the curt reply.

I suppose I said it all wrong but I wasn't much good at couching my thoughts in fine phrases.

'What's the matter with her?' I asked.

You could see her bristle. 'I don't think that's any business of yours,' was what she said. It was sharp. She thought I was just being nosy. She didn't understand that I loved Mrs Pearce. I missed her. She was the one natural-born teacher I ever knew. Without her my day had lost all its colour. There was just nothing to look forward to. Nobody compared with her. She was like a bus or a plane or a magic carpet. You sat down and she took you away.

Ages afterwards I heard it was lung cancer. But I didn't know that then. Anyway she never came back to school.

I carried my picture of Popocatepetl round with me for months, always hoping to hear the flappy sandals coming down the corridor. They never did. So you see she was only there for a little while. But what she did lasted much longer. Every time I was given a roneo'd sheet to name the rivers on, every time I shaded in the coalfields, every time I got bored doing diagrams of precipitation (why didn't they just say rain?) I knew that thanks to her, by just gazing away out of the window, I could see the lush jungles of Ecuador, the hard-baked plains of Mexico or, far away in the snow, the lights of a tiny house twinkling high on the mountains above Innsbruck.

# Crisis of Confidence

## A Sketch

*Played by two voices which represent both halves of the same person. The first voice is adventurous and optimistic, ready for anything. The other is the voice of caution, the one which casts doubt and persuades us against ever taking the bold course. To signify this, there is an* UP VOICE *and a* DOWN VOICE. *This could be performed by one actress playing both parts, or by placing her in the foreground with a shadowy, barely seen figure speaking in the background.*

*A single woman at home alone:*

## Part One: The Train

UP VOICE: I think I'll go out! Yep, I'll go out for a *change*. I just feel in the *mood*! That's it, I've decided, I'm going *out*.

DOWN VOICE: Where?

UP VOICE: What?

DOWN VOICE: Where? Where're you going?

UP VOICE (*spoilt for choice, wildly enthusiastic*): Oh yes, well ... um, where shall I *go*! I know! I'll go to London! I'll go and see *The Phantom of the Opera*. Oh, it's great, you know. *(Sings)* 'He's here, the phantom of the OpraAAA.' It's fantastic. I'll get my glad rags on, I've got a new dress, I'm GOING!

DOWN VOICE: How're you getting home?

UP VOICE: What?

DOWN VOICE: After the show. How're you getting home?

UP VOICE: Oh, I don't know ... the train! I'll come on the train, they do a late one for theatregoers.

DOWN VOICE: Oh, right. It comes ... all the way home ... does it?

UP VOICE: Well, not *all* the way. Not quite *all* the way.

DOWN VOICE: Oh. How far does it bring you?

UP VOICE: Well, to Kemble. My home station.

DOWN VOICE: Kemble.

UP VOICE: Yes.

DOWN VOICE: Do you think there'll be others coming back from *The Phantom of the Opera* to ... er ... Kemble?

UP VOICE: Well, I don't know. Probably not to Kemble *itself*.

DOWN VOICE: No. But it'd be a modern train, wouldn't it? It wouldn't be one of those without a corridor. You know, where you can get ... shut in ... with somebody.

UP VOICE: No. Well, they do have those sometimes. Occasionally. Quite often.

DOWN VOICE: You ever hear of the Kemble Mince Murderer?

UP VOICE: No!

DOWN VOICE: No, well it was a long time ago ... *(aside)* although he was never caught. Anyway once you reached Kemble you'd be fine wouldn't you? I expect it's all brightly lit, station buffets, bags of people, apple-cheeked station masters ... hawkers ...

UP VOICE: No.

DOWN VOICE: No?

UP VOICE: S'not manned after half-past five.

DOWN VOICE: Oh. Any lights? Lights in the car park?

UP VOICE: Just the one.

DOWN VOICE: And, of course, Kemble being very low-lying, you get a lot of FOG. You know, late at night, fog, a yellow halo round the one ... street ... light.

UP VOICE *(picturing all this)*: Nah. I don't fancy it. I don't think I'm going to go.

DOWN VOICE: That's a pity. You'd have enjoyed it.

## Part Two: The Coach

UP VOICE: I know! I could go on the coach. There's a good coach service and it's cheap! They have toilets ... and hostesses ... they've got a little bar at the back where you can buy a drink or have a cup of tea.

DOWN VOICE: Oh, really? That sounds nice.

UP VOICE: Yes. It would bring me back almost to the door.

DOWN VOICE: Oh, lovely. But could you find it after the show? What if you came out of the theatre and it's NOT THERE? I heard about a woman once, came out of the theatre, walked three streets trying to find it and all the time it had GONE WITHOUT HER!

UP VOICE *(firmly)*: No, it parks across the road. You can see it waiting.

DOWN VOICE *(momentarily stumped)*: But has it got seatbelts?

UP VOICE: Yes.

DOWN VOICE: Sure?

UP VOICE: YES! It's GOT seatbelts. Look, you keep putting me off! I'd never go anywhere if I listened to you. Those coaches are nice. They're very comfortable. They've got nice plush seats.

DOWN VOICE: With ashtrays on the back. Do you smoke?

UP VOICE: No, I don't smoke.

DOWN VOICE: No. I mean you wouldn't want to sit next to a smoker. A chain-smoker ... coughing. I knew a chain-smoker once, he coughed so much he coughed up a ...

UP VOICE: YES, thank you.

DOWN VOICE: Well, it gave *him* a shock. But then, that's not the *main* reason that most people choose to go by coach.

UP VOICE: No? What is it then?

DOWN VOICE: Well, most people travel by coach because they don't want to drive home. And they don't *want* to drive home because they intend to drink a lot. They want to go out and get ABSOLUTELY PLASTERED, and not have to drive home.

UP VOICE *(exasperated)*: Well, *I* don't have to sit by anybody like that!

DOWN VOICE: Ah, but you might not have a choice. The hostess might just lead him down the bus, here he comes look, he's got a drink still in his hand, he's swaying from side to side, leering, can't focus his eyes, he's got a red face, a great big beer gut, he's scratching himself and the ONE VACANT SEAT LEFT IS RIGHT NEXT TO ...

UP VOICE *(panic stricken)*: He's not sitting next to me!

## Part Three: The Car

UP VOICE: I know! I'll take my car! That's it, I'll drive. Easy. I'll set off in good time, park in the NCP near the friendly attendant and that'll be it. I'll be independent.

DOWN VOICE: Have you heard about those roaming gangs who attack people stopped at traffic lights?

UP VOICE: Yes. Well, I've got a rape alarm.

DOWN VOICE: Ah ... but they wear ear plugs. *(Helpfully)* You know, some people take a STUFFED MAN.

UP VOICE: A what?

DOWN VOICE: A stuffed man. A dummy to look like a companion. It's like a great big dolly. You put a hat on it. Stick a pipe in its mouth. Then in the darkness, you see, it looks like a person. It looks as if you're with ...

UP VOICE: Sherlock Holmes. I'm not mucking about like that! I've gone off the whole idea. I was looking forward to it but you've put me right off the whole thing.

DOWN VOICE: Well, DON'T BLAME ME! I was ONLY THINKING OF YOU. I mean, you wouldn't like it if you broke down. What if you broke down on the M25? All those lanes. All those cars thundering past. It wouldn't be very nice, a woman on her own. Ask yourself. Read the papers.

UP VOICE: Well, how much *is* a stuffed man?

DOWN VOICE: A hundred and fifty pounds.

UP VOICE: No, I'm not going! It's too much trouble. I'm not going. I'll stay round here.

DOWN VOICE: Oh, what a shame. You'd have had a nice night out.

## Part Four: The Sports Centre

UP VOICE: I've got it. I'll go down the sports centre for a swim. I haven't had a swim for ages. At least I know my way around down there. I can walk, I won't have to worry about the car, it's just round the corner. I know all the ropes. You go in, they're ever so friendly, you give them the money and they give you a key. That's what I'll do. And it's not one of those horrible communal changing rooms either, you get your own private cubicle, with a curtain.

DOWN VOICE: Then what happens?

UP VOICE: Well, you get undressed, put your swimsuit on, put your clothes in a locker, you've got the key on a rubber band and you put that on your wrist, and then you walk out.

DOWN VOICE: Where?

UP VOICE: What?

DOWN VOICE: Where do you walk?

UP VOICE: Well, you walk through the footbath, out through the arch and there's the pool...

DOWN VOICE: Yes ...

UP VOICE (*she is imagining it*): ... and everybody turns and STARES at you.

DOWN VOICE: Still, you shouldn't worry. Men like a BIT EXTRA. And I've always thought you look good in that swimsuit. It's marvellous how it's LASTED.

UP VOICE: Mmmmm. I dunno.

DOWN VOICE: Well, perhaps you can hop in the pool real quick, before anybody starts to laugh. Where are the steps down into the water?

UP VOICE (*wretchedly*): Right over the far side of the pool. I shall have to walk all the way round. In full view. Oh I'm not GOING swimming. I'm fed up. I'll just stay at home. I'll put on my comfy old dressing gown and curl up on the sofa with a book.

DOWN VOICE: What sofa?

UP VOICE: What do you mean, what sofa? I've only got one sofa.

DOWN VOICE: No, it's just that it's under the window. I wondered if you pruned that creeper. The one that TAPS ON THE GLASS. It's only that you'll be here on your own, and if there's a wind it always taps ... There IS a wind tonight. I expect you remembered and pruned it ages ago.

UP VOICE: No, I didn't prune it. I forgot.

DOWN VOICE: Well, I don't suppose it matters. It would only matter to a nervous person. And you're not a nervous person are you? Although there have been a lot of break-ins round here. Myself, I wouldn't BLAME a person for being nervous. (*Brightening*) But I think things like the wind outside, or plants tapping on the window, only affect you if you're reading a frightening kind of book. I don't suppose you are, are you? Reading a frightening book? I expect it's one about gardening. Or a historical romance, what do they call them, bodice rippers? (*Laughs. Laugh gradually peters out.*) What *is* the title of your book?

UP VOICE: *The Bloody Axe.* Oh this is hopeless! Now you've talked me out of THAT as well. All right, I won't go on the train, I won't go on the coach, I won't take my car, I won't go swimming, I won't read a book, what SHALL I do? WHAT SHALL I DO? What about watching telly? Is that SAFE? Will that suit you? I'll sit here all night and watch telly. I won't even make myself a cup of cocoa in case the cooker goes up in a

SHEET OF FLAME. Come on, you know it all! What IS on the telly?

DOWN VOICE: *The Revenge of Frankenstein.*

UP VOICE: I think *I'll* go and see *The Phantom of the Opera.*

# At the Hairdresser's

## A Sketch

### SCENE

*The interior of a high street unisex hairdresser's.*

### CHARACTERS

JULIE: *a hairdresser in her early twenties. She must know the basic techniques of cutting hair so that she is sectioning, cutting and checking the client's hair throughout. She is determined to hold a conversation with the client.*

THE CLIENT, MR BURGESS: *a man who was hoping to sit quietly and read his newspaper.*

### PROPS

FOR JULIE: *comb, hairdresser's scissors, mirror and large protective cape. A water sprayer, hair-sectioning clips and a brush for removing hair from the neckline. A substantial tuft of fake hair in colour to match client's. (This tuft of hair is taken from Julie's pocket, and concealed at the back of client's neck when she is tucking in his cape.)*

FOR MR BURGESS: *a newspaper.*

MR BURGESS *enters hairdresser's,* JULIE *approaches.*

JULIE: Hello, are you Mr Burgess? For 2.30?

CLIENT: Yes. Hello.

*Julie leads him to chair.*

JULIE: Right, if you'd like to take a seat. I don't believe we've seen you here before?

CLIENT: No, it's my first visit.

JULIE: Oh, that's why it is then. How are you today?

CLIENT: Oh, not very well, my dog died and I ...

JULIE *(she is not listening)*: Good. I'll just pop this around you. *(Billows the cape around him.)* After all, we don't want to give you a hairy chest! *(Laughs at pathetic joke.)* Just a tidy up today is it?

CLIENT *(he does not want a tidy up at all)*: No, I'd like it left longer at the sides, a little fuller at the back, spiked in front and layered over the ears please.

JULIE: Right. Just a tidy up then. *(She lifts a section of hair suspiciously.)* Who cut it before?

CLIENT: Frederick's. In the High Street.

JULIE *(with contempt)*: Yes. I thought as much. *(She takes up water sprayer and sprays his hair vigorously.)* What's the weather like?

CLIENT: It's raining.

JULIE *(still spraying him)*: It's what?

CLIENT *(engulfed in mist)*: It's raining.

JULIE: Oh. Still raining. Got a day off today then?

CLIENT: Yes.

JULIE: Had your holidays?

CLIENT: Yes.

JULIE: Did you go somewhere nice?

CLIENT: I went to Greece. To Rhodes.

JULIE: Oh. Where the chickens come from.

CLIENT: No, I think that's in America ...

JULIE *(interrupting)*: My boyfriend went to Greece. He
  didn't like it.

CLIENT *(not remotely interested)*: No?

JULIE: No. He said it was riddled with crime. RIDDLED.
  There was this poor woman in the apartment next to
  him and do you know what happened?

CLIENT *(he couldn't care less)*: No.

JULIE: Well, she was walking along to the market. Just
  minding her own business, walking along to the market
  and guess what?

CLIENT *(heavily)*: It was shut.

JULIE: No. Two men came up behind her on a moped with
  a great big knife, slashed the strap of her shoulder bag
  caught it and drove off. They got away with all her
  traveller's cheques, money, passport, everything. It
  ruined her holiday.

  *(There is a pained silence from client.)*

They just came up behind her with this great big knife. Slash!

*(She is quite carried away and makes a wild slashing gesture with the scissors, accidentally cutting off a sizeable handful of hair. It is, of course, the fake hair; She examines it guiltily, shrugs and tosses it away. Client, reading, does not realise.)*

AND he said the food was too oily. They have this feeta cheese. FEETA cheese, with all oil tipped on it. Chunks of feeta cheese with oil on. Well it wouldn't do for me. *(Inspects hair closely.)* Your hair's a bit oily.

CLIENT: Is it?

JULIE: Yes. D'you use a lot of mousse?

CLIENT: What? No.

JULIE: How about gel?

CLIENT: No.

JULIE: Do you work indoors?

CLIENT: Yes, I do mostly.

JULIE: That'd be it then. What do you do?

CLIENT: I'm a musician.

JULIE: Oh, are you? That's nice. I like music. My uncle plays the mouth organ.

CLIENT: No, I'm a professional musician.

JULIE: My uncle once stood next to Luciano Pavarotti. He got his mouth organ out but Pavarotti just walked away. He wore a wig.

CLIENT: Pavarotti?

JULIE: No, my uncle. It was nylon. I mean, it looked all right from the front, but the back was like Davy Crockett's hat. Still, he was like you, he couldn't half play the mouth organ.

CLIENT (*growing desperate*): But I don't play the ...

JULIE (*she is oblivious to him*): My boyfriend's a tiler. He's just been tiling this woman's house down the bypass. She spent two thousand pounds on hand-made tiles for her kitchen. My boyfriend said they was nothin' special. Nothin' special at all. They just had a few speckles and spots on! (*Finds something in his hair.*) You've got a spot here.

CLIENT: Have I?

JULIE: It's all right. I'll go round it. Have you come far?

CLIENT: No.

JULIE: Have a good Christmas?

CLIENT: Yes.

JULIE: Going out tonight?

CLIENT: No.

JULIE: Go out last night?

CLIENT: No.

JULIE: Going out tomorrow night?

CLIENT: No.

JULIE: Kids've gone back to school.

CLIENT: Yes.

JULIE: Do you live round here then?

CLIENT: No.

JULIE: I live up by the Mosque.

*(Irritated silence from client.)*

Up by the Mosque I live.

CLIENT: Amazing.

JULIE: It's a lovely building, made of white marble. It reminds me of the Raj Mahal. It's just down our road. It's lovely. It's got a high wall all round it and then out of the top it's got this huge white dome. This huge white dome growing out of the top of it ... You've got a bald spot here.

CLIENT: Oh no!

JULIE: You think you've got problems. You should have seen the woman we had in here last week.

CLIENT: Oh?

JULIE: Her hair was *(lowers voice and speaks with relish)* crawlin'. It was crawling. Didn't realise. We had to fumigate.

CLIENT *(horrified)*: Fumigate? *(Scratches himself surreptitiously.)*

JULIE: Mmmmm. *(Pause)* Do you smoke?

CLIENT: Smoke? No.

JULIE: My boyfriend smokes. I tell him not to but he says he needs the matches for spacers.

CLIENT: Spacers?

JULIE: To stick in between the tiles. It holds them apart
before he grouts. We've got terrible trouble with the
grouting in our bathroom. It's got a horrible black
fungi growing on it. A black, creeping, greasy fungi.
Cup of coffee?

CLIENT: No thank you.

JULIE: Cup of tea?

CLIENT: No thank you.

JULIE: Jacket potato?

CLIENT: NO THANK YOU!

JULIE: You *are* being good. *(This reminds her of her
lifelong preoccupation – dieting.)* I was good all day
yesterday. I only had cottage cheese. Oh and a banana.
June brought these bananas in. She's on this banana
diet. She's lost four pounds. She has to have bananas
for breakfast, bananas for dinner, bananas for tea. Then
if she wants a snack in the evening, guess what she has
to have?

CLIENT *(this is driving him nuts)*: Steak and chips!

JULIE *(brightly)*: No! Another banana!

*(Client, in despair, looks at his watch. Julie finishes.)*

JULIE: There we are then.

*(She brushes him off and picks up the mirror,)*

Let me just show you the back. All right? Do you like
it?

*(She flashes the mirror round the back of his head so fast that he cannot possibly see anything.)*

CLIENT *(leadenly)*: Yes, thank you.

JULIE: Oh, good. You see I always try to match the style of the hair to the personality of the face.

*(Aside)* 'Course, sometimes you don't have all that much to work with.

Right! Well if you'd just like to come to the desk. It's been lovely talking to you. Really interesting. And just so I can tell my uncle, whereabouts ARE you playing the mouth organ?

*BLACKOUT*

# Chrysanths Are Always Nice

## A Sketch

*The interior of a high street flower shop,* JOANNA, *the shop assistant, is seated at a desk. On the desk are a telephone, a pad of order forms and a ring-binder file. The telephone rings and* JOANNA *answers it. It is clear that she has said the preliminaries many times before.*

JOANNA: Good afternoon, Phone a Flower, Joanna speaking, how may I help you?

Oh yes, we do *send* flowers. We have a delivery service in our own area or else we telegraph.

Well, we do bouquet, arrangement, posy, spray or dried.

No, DRIED not died.

The minimum charge is twenty-five pounds, sir. This includes cellophane wrap, appropriate embellishments and lavish ribboning. Then you get a few flowers under all that.

Did you have any particular flowers in mind? Spring flowers for instance, or I can select them for you, for colour, fragrance or longevity.

Well, it means how long they stand up. Before they fall down.

Oh yes, *I'd* say they would be a very good choice. Chrysanths are always nice. You can't go wrong with chrysanths and today I have got some of the Bronze.

Oh good. Now, how would you like to pay? We accept Access, Visa, American Express, Diners, Barclaycard, Switch, Swipe, Account or money.

Yes, we accept that one.

May I have the number?

Your name as it appears on the card?

The expiry date?

Your postcode?

And your blood group.

Thank you. Now, can you give me the name and address of the recipient?

Well. Who's going to get it?

I'm sorry, which ward was that? Yes. The Royal Infirmary. Right. And what message would you like to send with your flowers?

No, we don't specify the number of words but the length of message is governed by the dimensions of the card.

By how big it is. So ... what would you like to say?

No, no, don't feel rushed. It *is* difficult. Lots of people have to have a little think about this part. Is it for the birth of a baby?

Ah. It's a man.

Oh yes, I'm sure a man would like chrysanths. And they last for ages, you know. How ill is he?

Oh good. So ... what would you like to say on the card?

No, I don't think you're stupid at all. Lots of people find it hard with the words.

Well, my advice is don't have anything too serious. You just want a get-well message, something to cheer him up. If you like I'll read you a few of the other messages, and you can see if anything gives you an idea. No, I don't mind at all. Hold on, I'll just get my file ...

*(She leafs through the ring-binder file.)*

*(Reassuringly)* Oh, we've got all sorts here, I'm sure we'll be able to find just the thing. There's even one for 'Good Luck in Your Exam!' *(She reads)*

> Against your every answer,
> May the teacher place a tick,
> And if by chance he doesn't,
> Well you can't *help* being thick.

Or this one on Retirement:

> Your steady grip upon the rudder's easing,
> The ship of life, with you upon the prow,
> Is heaving-to at last, in calmer waters,
> In other waters, you're on the scrap heap now.

No, I'm sorry, you did say Get Well. Look, here's one!

> I hope you are recovered,
> And your legs are out of plaster,
> Your wife's moved in with me
> So don't get better any faster.

No, that wouldn't do at all. How about this one?

> Be sure to take your medicine,
> And eat your par-boiled egg,
> We miss you more than words can say,
> Get well soon. Break a leg.

Yes, it's rather nice. Sort of theatrical. That one then? Thank you, I always try to be helpful. I'll just add on the delivery charge, service charge, transmission charge and the shop identification and that will go out this afternoon. Thank you so much. You're welcome. Bye!

*(She muses to herself, browsing through the file.)*

Well, I thought I managed that very well. I'm only sorry he wasn't getting married or I could have suggested this one here!

> Good luck on your wedding day,
> I think you're bold and plucky,
> And as the other two have failed,
> Let's hope it's third time lucky!

*(She rises from the desk.)*

Right. Where's the chrysanths? Chrysanths are always nice.

*(She walks briskly offstage to her workroom.)*